Targeting LISTENING and SPEAKING

Strategies and Activities for ESL/EFL Students

Keith S. Folse, Ph.D.
M.A. TESOL Program
University of Central Florida

Darren Bologna
English Language Institute
Kanda University of International Studies, Japan

THE UNIVERSITY OF MICHIGAN PRESS
Ann Arbor

Photos courtesy of Laramie Photography (Units 2–8)
and Kerri Kijewski (Unit 1). Illustrations courtesy
of Sarah Reaume.

Acknowledgments

No educator or materials writer works in a vacuum. How many students and teachers
have we worked with over the years that have influenced us in our teaching? These
students and teachers are the main people to be acknowledged here, for our work as
teachers and materials developers is a product of the influences and ideas of those we
have taught and worked with.

We would like to thank the many ESL/EFL professionals we have been in touch
with electronically through TESL-L, TESLMW-L, and TESLIE-L.

Finally, we would like to thank the staff at the University of Michigan Press for
their encouragement and hard work in the completion of this book. It is because of
their hard work that the University of Michigan Press continues to be a leader in ESL
teaching materials.

TO THE TEACHER

TEACHING LISTENING AND SPEAKING CLASSES

As a teacher, what do you do in a listening class? Or if you teach in an integrated program, what kinds of activities are good listening activities? And how does speaking or discussing interact with listening? Can you have listening that does not involve speaking or speaking that does not involve listening?

Some teachers find that it is certainly a challenge to teach listening and speaking. Learners need listening activities that give them an opportunity to hone their listening skills through focusing on both the larger message (*top-down activities*) and key words or phrases (*bottom-up activities*). In top-down activities, learners may listen for the gist or main idea of a message. In bottom-up activities, learners might have to identify a word as having a specific sound (/s/ vs. /z/, for example). In either case, what is most important is that learners have activities that are manageable, that is, at the correct student proficiency level of English, and that are short and focused.

No listening can happen without speaking, and no speaking can happen without listening. Therefore, it is only natural that a book that hones students' listening ability should include a large number of speaking activities. In a listening class, students need opportunities to listen to the recording and also to listen to each other.

The benefit of working with recorded activities should be obvious. The recording can be stopped at any point, and it can also be played numerous times so that students can focus in on both specific and general aspects of the message. These kinds of activities require active participation and attention on the learners' part in order to be completed successfully.

The benefit of speaking/discussing activities is that they provide learners with a chance to produce output in English. This output serves as input for their own language growth. In addition, this output is the basis of any negotiation of meaning with their fellow learners. Real learning will take place when students' communication breaks down due to mistakes in pronunciation or listening comprehension and learners then negotiate either within their own minds or with the other interlocutors to figure out what is happening. It is during this negotiation of meaning that the proverbial lightbulb comes on and learners make important realizations about aspects of their English. They notice the gap between what they were producing and what they should have been producing.

These speaking/discussion activities are highly interactive. All parties must participate or the activity cannot be completed. Let's use a tennis analogy, where the goal is to play against an unknown player who plays very well (i.e., the native speaker). Good players become good players by practicing with a ball machine or with a coach, hitting the same shot over and over until they almost perfect it. Some of these drills are easy; others are tough. Some we do only a few times; others we do numerous times. This is the equivalent to the listening practice that we have in recorded listening activities. In addition, good tennis players sometimes practice all of their shots with a hitting partner. Sometimes they hit with someone better for a challenge; other times they hit with someone slightly weaker to improve certain shots. This is the equivalent to the listening practice that occurs during a discussion or speaking activity.

In *Targeting Listening and Speaking*, we have included about 70 percent listening activities and 30 percent speaking activities. However, you should keep in mind that very few exercises are listening only or speaking only. In fact, nearly all activities practice both important skills.

TEXT ORGANIZATION

Targeting Listening and Speaking consists of eight units. Units 1–7 are new lessons, and Unit 8 is a test or comprehension check unit.

Each of the seven units has a general theme around which all exercises are built. Because the single most important nonlinguistic skill in ESL/EFL listening is *prediction*—i.e., the ability to anticipate what the speaker will say—having a theme for all the material in the unit helps learners make better predictions about what the recordings will say. The unit themes are:

Unit 1. Studying English
Unit 2. Food
Unit 3. Animals and Pets
Unit 4. Free Time and Hobbies
Unit 5. Spending Money
Unit 6. Family and Friends
Unit 7. Travel

Unit 8 consists of four listening tests. Each test has 25 multiple-choice items. We recommend that these tests be administered as a progress check every few weeks in the term. It is also possible to administer these tests as a pretest and posttest format. Teachers (and students) should remember that these tests are only one type of measure. We prefer to view these four tests as progress check opportunities rather than as tests since listening and speaking are true skills, when compared to more concrete, learnable language areas such as grammar and vocabulary. Thus, it is easier to test students' knowledge of newly acquired vocabulary than it is to do the same for listening growth.

TYPES OF INTERACTIONS IN THE EXERCISES

Units 1 through 7 have approximately 20 exercises per unit. In the following general format of a sample unit, the Ⓛ refers to a listening exercise, Ⓢ to a

Beginning of unit	• (L/S) Listening Activity
	• (L) Dictation in a Dialogue
	(L) Extra Practice. Listening Practice
	(S/L) Extra Practice. Dialogue Practice
	• (L) Skills
	• (L) Skills
	• (S/L) Speaking/Discussion (preparation)
	• (S/L) Speaking/Discussion
	• (L) Skills
	• (L) Skills
	• (S/L) Speaking/Discussion (preparation)
	• (S/L) Speaking/Discussion
	• (L) Understanding Simple Conversations
	• (L) Skills
	• (L) Skills
	• (L/S) Sound Practice: Minimal Pair Discrimination
	• (L/S) Sound Practice: Minimal Pairs in Sentences
	• (L) Understanding Simple Lectures
	• (S/L) Pair Talking
	• (S/L) Speaking/Discussion (preparation)
End of unit	• (S/L) Speaking/Discussion

speaking exercise, (L/S) to a listening activity that requires or fosters some speaking, and (S/L) to a speaking activity that requires listening on the speakers' parts.

Listening Activity

Units 1–7 each contain two exercises labeled **LISTENING ACTIVITY**. One of these opens each unit, and the other is about three-quarters of the way through the unit. In these activities, students will listen to language that explains an interesting situation or set of facts. In the unit on pets (Unit 3), for example, listeners will take a test about cat facts. The questions are spoken, but the answers are on the page. In the unit on travel (Unit 7), students will complete a quiz about the location of some of the top travel destinations in the world. After students have answered the questions and perhaps talked with other students, learners must listen to the information in order to check their responses. In other words, learners have a real reason for listening: Listening helps them to verify their answers.

Dictation in a Dialogue

We believe that dictation is a good thing. Students need to practice the details that come out through practice in dictation, e.g., did you say *he* or *she?* We do not, however, want to use dictation of isolated sentences. Listening very much involves prediction, and it is difficult to predict consistently without some sustained context. For these reasons, we offer a new twist on dictation, Dictation in a Dialogue.

In this exercise, two (or more) people are talking about something related to the theme of the unit, such as travel or spending money. Students see the entire dialogue written out **except for seven sentences**. These seven sentences have been replaced by longer blanks. Two numbers are connected to each blank. The number in front of the blank is the sentence number (1–7). The number after the blank is the number of words in the missing sentence.

Students will hear only the seven missing sentences on the tape. First, they'll hear number 1. Students will be told to listen and repeat the sentence. This is important for students to capture the sentence in short-term memory and replay it in their heads a time or two. Then number 1 will be read again, and students are to write the sentence that they hear. Again, students are encouraged to "hear" the sentence in their heads as they write it out. Then, after a short pause, students will hear the sentence a third time to check what they have written. The format is always: **listen/repeat**, **listen/write**, **listen/check**. This is done for all seven missing sentences.

Following this exercise are two EXTRA PRACTICE activities. The first is Extra Practice. Listening Practice. Here, students can hear the whole recording of the dictation practiced. We encourage students to attempt this without opening their books. You only have one chance to hear something for the first time. If students have their books open and read along the first time and then listen to the dialogue with books closed for the second round of listening, *it is not at all the same practice.* For this reason, we *strongly* recommend that students listen with their books closed the first, and maybe even the second, time in order to have real listening practice. Then we recommend having students follow along with books open if they wish.

The second activity is Extra Practice. Dialogue Practice. Students should take turns reading the dialogue out loud. They should work in pairs (or small groups). If students are working in threes and the dialogue has two people (person A and person B), then one person can read A, another can read B, and the other can listen with book closed. In the second practice, the person who only listened can read A, the person who read A before can read B, and now B can listen. In the third practice, students switch roles one more time. In this way, students have a chance to build fluency through consistent practice.

Skills

Each unit contains seven to ten Listening Skills exercises. With rare exception, these skills focus on bottom-up areas. Students work on listening for the difference in numbers (for example, 15 vs. 50) or the difference in names of letters (*E* vs. *I*) or in number at the sentence level (*He has a history book* vs. *He has some history books*).

If students have already completed a particular exercise but need further practice, they should write their answers on a sheet of paper. For example, if students are to tell if the sentence that they hear is affirmative or negative (*All of the cups are on the table* vs. *All of the cups aren't on the table*) by circling + for affirmative or – for negative, the teacher can have the students mark + or – on their own papers. Since the students will have the correct answers in their books from the first time that they did the exercise, the teacher can direct students to open their books to correct their own papers.

Speaking/Discussion Preparation and Speaking/Discussion

Each unit contains three interesting Speaking/Discussion Activities. We strongly believe that it is not good practice to give students a topic and ask them to discuss. Second language research shows that ESL learners produce more language and more targetlike language when the activity is a **closed task** (i.e., there is one or a limited set of answers), requires (not just encourages or hopes for but actually *requires*) an exchange of information, and contains a planning phase (instead of students just being confronted suddenly with a topic).

In the unit on spending money (Unit 5), for example, one of the speaking/discussion exercises asks students to come up with gift ideas for several people (e.g., your 88-year-old grandmother who has everything she needs or your boss who likes to read but whose reading taste you do not know well). Since the whole class will hear each group's ideas, students could vote on the best gift ideas. Because there would be one answer at the end, this could be a **closed** task.

Two of the three important aspects of speaking/discussion activities have been covered. The final one is Preparation. In this book, each speaking/ discussion exercise is preceded by a preparation exercise, in which students must read the problem and write out their answers. Again, second language research shows that students' performance is significantly different when students have a chance to plan their ideas and language. (For further information on this research and application to ESL materials, see the Preface in *Discussion Starters* [Folse 1995], *More Discussion Starters* [Folse and Ivone 2001], and *First Discussion Starters* [Folse and Ivone 2002].)

Preparation is extremely important for the success of a good listening-speaking class. The design of this exercise plays an important role in ensuring that students actually practice speaking *and* listening in this exercise. In addition, the topics used in this exercise are intriguing, and students will want more! For these reasons, each unit contains three speaking/discussion activities.

Understanding Simple Conversations

One of the more immediate goals of most ESL/EFL students is the ability to understand a conversation between two native speakers. In Understanding Simple Conversations, students listen to a conversation about a topic related to the general theme of the unit. In addition, a more specific idea of the conversation can be deduced from the title just after the exercise number at the beginning of the exercise. For example, the general theme of Unit 4 is Free Time and Hobbies, and the title of the Understanding Simple Conversations exercise is Free Time Plans. As might be expected from the title, the two people talk about what they are going to do in the near future. Because prediction plays such an important role in developing good listening skills, it is important for the teacher to help students make predictions that they can verify as they listen to the material. Teachers should not take this skill for granted. It is pedagogically sound to ask adults what they think the conversation will be about before playing the recording and then to discuss afterward why certain predictions were or were not realized in the recording.

After students listen to the material, they must then answer five to eight questions about the information.

Sound Practice

Each unit contains one or more exercises that focus on an individual sound or sound problem. The sounds presented are those encountered by a wide array of first language backgrounds, including speakers of Spanish, Korean, Japanese, Thai, Vietnamese, Arabic, Chinese, Portuguese, French, Russian, and German.

The sounds/problems covered are:

Unit 1: problem letters (**A/E, E/I, G/J, B/P, L/R, S/Z**)
Unit 2: problem letters (**A/E**), minimal pair—/s/ and /z/
Unit 3: problem letters (**E/I**), pronunciation of the ending *-s* (/s/, /z/, /ɪz/)
Unit 4: problem letters (**A/E/I**), pronunciation of the ending *-ed* (/d/, /t/, /ɪd/)
Unit 5: problem letters (common combinations), minimal pair—/b/ and /v/
Unit 6: problem syllables (*-teen/-ty*), minimal pair—/ch/ and /sh/
Unit 7: problem endings (*-st, -nd, -rd, -th*), minimal pair—/l/ and /r/

There are two minimal pair listening activities in units 3, 5, 6, and 7. In the first one, students hear one word that has one of the two sounds in it. The student book page has three sections for this exercise—beginning, middle, and end—to indicate where the sound in question occurs in the word. For example, in Unit 6 with the /ch/ and /sh/ pair, students hear "wish." On the blank, they must write *sh* to indicate that they have heard this sound. This exercise has twenty items, and each one-third of the items practices the sounds in the initial position, the middle position, or the final position. After the listening exercise, there is an expansion task, also divided by the beginning-middle-ending distinction, in which students are encouraged to come up with their own (and perhaps more relevant to them) examples.

In the second exercise, students see the two words with the minimal pair sounds, such as *cheese* and *she's*. Students first read the two words to themselves and then hear a complete sentence, which provides more real-world context to assist with listening. Students are asked to circle the word that they believe that they have heard.

Understanding Simple Lectures

Good listening skills must be applicable to a variety of types of listening. Listening only to other students about daily topics is one kind of listening. In this exercise, students listen to a monologue about a topic that is related to the general theme of the unit. Again, the title found next to the exercise number will help students in using schema knowledge to predict the information in this activity. Students listen to the material and then answer five to eight questions about the material. This activity helps prepare students in academic settings for more rigorous listening tasks.

Pair Talking

In this exercise, students must describe people and things in illustrations so that the listener is able to identify which picture is being described. Students work in pairs. Student A works on one page, and student B works on the next page. It is important that students not look at each other's page.

Pair Talking always has six questions, and each question consists of four illustrations that have similar visual cues (each of the four pictures has some of the same people and a tree, but the placement of the people around the tree varies) or linguistically (there is ice in one picture; in another there are eyes). In other words, the pictures are very good distractors to make careful explanation of the details more necessary for the student to be able to identify the exact picture that the partner is describing.

Student A describes questions 1, 3, and 5. On student A's page, numbers 1, 3, and 5 already have a picture marked with a black dot. Student A must describe the picture with the dot well enough so that student B can put a dot by the exact same picture. Student B is encouraged to ask as many questions as possible at the same time to ascertain which picture is being described. Student B does the same thing with questions 2, 4, and 6.

Though the four pictures for any number (question) are the same four pictures, they are in different order on student A's page than they are on student B's page. If not, students could just say, "It's the second picture." In this way, students must really describe the picture, not its location on the page, and that need helps build fluency.

Rapid Vocabulary Review

One of the single most important aspects of building better listening ability in any second language is vocabulary growth. Knowledge of many individual vocabulary items—including words, phrases, idioms, expressions, and whole sentences—is crucial. Not knowing a few words in a passage might *hinder* comprehension; not knowing enough vocabulary or certain key vocabulary will *prevent* comprehension.

A unique feature is Rapid Vocabulary Review, which at the end of each unit of *Targeting Listening and Speaking* contains 25 multiple-choice vocabulary items.

Each unit in this book also has five additional vocabulary recycling activities that can be found on the companion Web site (www.press.umich.edu/esl/compsite/targetinglistening/). We strongly urge students to take advantage of these activities and record their scores in their books.

Vocabulary learning is essential to better listening skills.

Answer Key and Script

Both the answer key and script are available on the companion Web site for this book: (www.press.umich.edu/esl/compsite/targetinglistening/).

CONTENTS

Unit 3   Theme: Animals and Pets

Unit 6   Theme: Family and Friends

Studying English

Listening Activity: Completing a Class Schedule

Look at the schedule below. This is a schedule for all of the English classes that meet on Tuesdays and Thursdays at Valencia College. This schedule has the name of the course, the section number, the days, the time, the room number, and the instructor's name.

Some of the information is missing from the schedule. Listen carefully and fill in the missing numbers in this schedule.

CLASS SCHEDULE: ENGLISH TUESDAY–THURSDAY CLASSES					
COURSE	SECTION	DAYS	TIME	ROOM NO.	INSTRUCTOR
English 1	001	Tues/Thurs	8:00–9:10	414	Smith
English 1		Tues/Thurs	2:00–3:10		Kim
English 1		Tues/Thurs			Langston
	008	Tues/Thurs			Fletcher
English 2		Tues/Thurs		302	Rowen
English 2		Tues/Thurs	10:00–11:10		Blackwell
English 3	005	Tues/Thurs			Hardy
English 3		Tues/Thurs			Sommers
	001	Tues/Thurs			Martinez

Exercise
2

Dictation in a Dialogue: Students Discussing English Classes

This dialogue happens at a language school. The people in the dialogue are four students.

There are seven blank lines in the dialogue. Begin by filling in each blank line with the correct sentence that you will hear.

Listen carefully. First, you will hear a number. Find that sentence number. You will hear each sentence three times. Listen to the sentence. Then repeat the sentence. Then listen again. Write the sentence. Finally, listen again. Check your sentence. The number in parentheses is the number of words in the sentence. Now let's begin with number 1.

Diana: Lim, how many years do people study English in China?

Lim: In China, it depends on the school. ❶ _____

_____ . (11)

What about in Colombia?

Diana: In Colombia, most students in good schools study English for six years. Some people study English for eight years.

Lim: ❷ _____ ? (5)
Now I understand why. Ahmed, what about in Egypt?

Ahmed: ❸ _____ ? (5)
Some schools don't have English classes.

❹ _____ ? (6)

Diana: That sounds similar to what happens in Colombia.

Kumiko: ❺ _____ ? (6)

Ahmed: ❻ _____ ? (4)

Kumiko: For a long time, there were only three years of English classes. Now some schools offer six, eight, ten, or even twelve years of English.

Lim: Wow! ❼ _____ ? (5)

Kumiko: Yes, it is. Maybe in the near future Japanese high school students will speak English better.

Listening Practice

Close your books. Now listen to the complete dialogue from Exercise 2. If there is any part that you cannot understand well, listen to that part again. (Try to listen to this dialogue without looking at your book. This is a good way to improve your listening.)

Dialogue Practice

Work in groups of four. Look at Exercise 2 again. Each person will be one of the characters in the dialogue. Read the dialogue as the characters. When you have finished, change characters and read it again. After you have finished, you may want to listen to the recording of the dialogue one more time.

Numbers 1–20	
1 one	11 eleven
2 two	12 twelve
3 three	13 thirteen
4 four	14 fourteen
5 five	15 fifteen
6 six	16 sixteen
7 seven	17 seventeen
8 eight	18 eighteen
9 nine	19 nineteen
10 ten	20 twenty

Exercise 3

Number Practice: 1–10

Listen carefully. You will hear one sentence. Each sentence has a number in it. Write the number in numeral form that you hear.

Example: YOU HEAR: "Joe has four books."

ANSWER: Joe has __4__ books.

1. Our grammar class is at noon, but the vocabulary class is at _____ o'clock.

2. A multiple-choice question usually has _____ choices: A, B, C, or D.

3. A week has _____ days.

4. A student in middle school might be _____ years old.

5. Some countries like the Philippines have long names, but India has only _____ letters in it.

6. This is a very tough class. The students have to read _____ book every week.

7. _____ of the students in this class are married. All the others are single.

8. He speaks _____ languages: French, Spanish, Japanese, and Arabic.

9. In the class, we usually work in groups of _____ students.

10. Dr. Brown teaches _____ classes in the morning. His other classes are in the afternoon.

11. What is the best way to get to the main office from here? Actually, there are _____ ways to get there.

12. Paraguay is a country in South America. The word **Paraguay** has _____ letters in it.

13. It is good if _____ students work together to try to find the answer to the problem.

14. Every student has a different schedule. For example, I have _____ classes every day.

15. The main vowels in English are **A, E, I, O,** and **U.** If you count the letter **Y,** then there are _____ vowels in English.

Exercise
4

Number Practice: 11–20

Listen carefully. You will hear one sentence. Each sentence has a number in it. Write the number in numeral form that you hear.

Example: YOU HEAR: "Sue has fourteen books."

ANSWER: Sue has _14_ books.

1. The report for the history class has to be at least _____ pages long.

2. There are three high schools in my town. From my house, it takes exactly _____ minutes to walk to Boone High School.

3. She is in great shape. She spends about _____ hours every week at the gym.

4. The math test is usually short. It has only _____ questions.

5. Our conversation class is not so big. It has only _____ students in it.

6. My French class starts at _____ o'clock.

7. This exercise is longer than the last exercise. This exercise has _____ questions.

8. Most students in my class are _____ years old.

9. You can find a map of North America, Central America, and South America on page _____ .

10. The business section of the newspaper has _____ pages.

11. If you have _____ dollars, you can buy that book.

12. These coins add up to _____ cents.

13. A dozen is ———— .

14. A few of the students are absent today, so there are only ————

    students in class now.

15. Your score is 75 because you have only ———— answers that are

    correct.

Exercise 5

Number Practice: 1–20

Listen carefully. You will hear one sentence. Each sentence has a number in it. Write the number in numeral form that you hear.

Example: YOU HEAR: "I study about sixteen hours per week."

ANSWER: I study about _16_ hours per week.

1. The most difficult question on the quiz is question number _____ .

2. What time does your math class begin? Mine begins at _____

   o'clock.

3. Students from _____ schools will attend the meeting tomorrow.

4. My French class finishes at _____ o'clock.

5. Your French class ends at _____ o'clock.

6. My history class has _____ students.

7. Your history class is smaller. It has only _____ students.

8. In this classroom, there are only _____ desks.

9. Dozen means _____ .

10. The teacher said, "Please study page _____ tonight."

11. In many countries, it is not good luck to use the number _____ .

12. In this exercise, question number _____ is difficult.

13. In this exercise, question number _____ is easy.

14. In this exercise, question number _____ is long.

15. In this exercise, question number _____ is short.

Exercise
6

Speaking/Discussion: What Is a Good Teacher?

Practice 6A. Preparation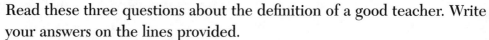

Read these three questions about the definition of a good teacher. Write your answers on the lines provided.

1. Who was the best teacher that you have ever had? What class was it? When was this?

_____

_____

_____

_____

2. Why was this teacher so good?

_____

_____

_____

_____

3. Can you make some general statements about what a good teacher is? What are three or four qualities of a good teacher?

   a. _____

   _____

   b. _____

   _____

   c. _____

   _____

   d. _____

   _____

Practice 6B. Group Speaking/Discussion

Now work with a partner or in a group of three to four students. Take turns discussing your responses to the questions in Practice 6A.

Alphabet		
A a	J j	S s
B b	K k	T t
C c	L l	U u
D d	M m	V v
E e	N n	W w
F f	O o	X x
G g	P p	Y y
H h	Q q	Z z
I i	R r	

Exercise
7

Recognizing Alphabet Letters

Listen carefully. You will hear one letter. Write the letter that you hear.

Example: YOU HEAR: "S"

ANSWER: S

1. ——   11. ——

2. ——   12. ——

3. ——   13. ——

4. ——   14. ——

5. ——   15. ——

6. ——   16. ——

7. ——   17. ——

8. ——   18. ——

9. ——   19. ——

10. ——   20. ——

Understanding Simple Conversations: Students and Classes

You will hear a short conversation between two students. They are talking about their classes this semester. Listen carefully. After you hear the conversation, read the questions below. Put a check (✓) by the correct answer.

1. What does Susan think about Joe's class?
   ____ a. She does not agree with Joe.
   ____ b. Joe has a good book for his grammar class.
   ____ c. The teacher asks the students to do a lot of work.

2. What time did the conversation begin?
   ____ a. 2:15   ____ b. 1:50   ____ c. 11:15

3. In the conversation, they talked about the library because
   ____ a. Joe works there part-time.
   ____ b. Susan has a class there.
   ____ c. Mr. Lucas has a book for Susan there.

4. What does Joe dislike about his class?
   ____ a. the book
   ____ b. the days of the class
   ____ c. the homework

5. Joe has class on
   ____ a. Tuesday.   ____ b. Wednesday.   ____ c. Thursday.

6. What is Susan going to do now?
   ____ a. walk to her class
   ____ b. study in the library
   ____ c. do her homework

7. Lucas is the last name of
   ____ a. the teacher.   ____ b. Susan.   ____ c. Joe.

8. What do we know about their classes?
   ____ a. They are studying grammar, but they are in different classes.
   ____ b. They are in different grammar classes, but they have the same teacher.
   ____ c. Their classes are in the library, but they are on different days.

Directions (Instructions)

Here are some examples of common directions:

1. **Write**	"Write the letter **F**."	_____	
2. **Circle**	"Circle the letter **F**."	B D F	
3. **Underline**	"Underline the letter **F**."	B D F	
4. **Spell**	"Spell the word *cat*."	_____	
5. **Check (✓)**	"Put a check by the letter **F**."	B ___	
		D ___	
		F ___	

Exercise 9

Understanding Simple Directions

Listen carefully. You will hear directions for the ten problems in this exercise. You will put a circle, underline, write the answer, or put a check. Listen to the directions carefully.

Example: YOU HEAR: "Write the word **books.**"

          ANSWER: ___books___

1. _____   6. __ 2 __ 7 __ 17

2. 13   15   17   7. _____

3. F   G   H   8. __ D __ N __ V

4. _____   9. 4   8   12

5. _____   10. W   T   E

Exercise 10

Understanding Simple Directions

Listen carefully. You will hear directions for the ten problems in this exercise. You will put a circle, underline, write the answer, or put a check. Listen to the directions carefully.

Example: YOU HEAR: "Circle the word that is an animal."

          ANSWER: truck (horse) lemon

1. L   C   A   6. _____

2. _____   7. K   Z   C

3. 2   11   20   8. __ A __ Y __ H

4. _____   9. 14   16   18

5. __ 1 __ 11 __ 17   10. _____

Exercise 11

Speaking/Discussion: Education

Practice 11A. Preparation

Read these statements and indicate your reactions by circling

① if you agree strongly,
② if you agree,
③ if you are not sure,
④ if you disagree, and
⑤ if you disagree strongly.

Then write your opinions or explanations on the lines below.

a.   1 2 3 4 5   Education from kindergarten to university should be free.

_____

_____

_____

_____

b.   1 2 3 4 5   Today's students are not as smart as they were in the past.

_____

_____

_____

_____

c.   1 2 3 4 5   Today's teachers are not as well prepared to teach as they were in the past.

_____

_____

_____

_____

d.   1 2 3 4 5   University students should receive a salary
                       from the government.

_____

_____

_____

_____

e.   1 2 3 4 5   Most students do not like tests, but tests are
                       a necessary part of education.

_____

_____

_____

_____

f.   1 2 3 4 5   Students who do not make a passing grade
                       should not be allowed to continue in public
                       education.

_____

_____

_____

_____

Practice 11B. Group Speaking/Discussion

Now work with a partner or in a group of three to four students. Take
turns discussing your responses to the questions in Practice 11A.

Practice with Confusing Letters

Listen carefully. In this exercise, you will practice some difficult and confusing letters of the English alphabet. You will hear each letter one time. Look at the three letters. Choose the correct letter that you hear and put a check (✓) by the correct letter.

Example: YOU HEAR: "Z"

ANSWER: __ C   __ S   ✓ Z

1. __ B   __ P   __ V   11. __ G   __ J   __ Y

2. __ A   __ E   __ I   12. __ U   __ W   __ Q

3. __ M   __ N   __ L   13. __ S   __ F   __ C

4. __ D   __ T   __ Z   14. __ O   __ U   __ A

5. __ R   __ L   __ E   15. __ I   __ A   __ E

6. __ C   __ Z   __ G   16. __ L   __ R   __ W

7. __ B   __ V   __ P   17. __ G   __ Y   __ J

8. __ I   __ E   __ A   18. __ K   __ Q   __ U

9. __ H   __ J   __ G   19. __ X   __ H   __ S

10. __ A   __ E   __ I   20. __ G   __ Y   __ J

Exercise
13

Listening Activity: Class List of Students

This is a list of students who are taking English I this spring semester. This list is for section 001, which meets on Monday, Wednesday, and Friday from 8 A.M. to 9:15 A.M. Look at this class list. It gives the student number; the student's name, sex, age, and country of origin; and the number of years that the student has studied English. Some of the information is missing from the schedule. Listen carefully and fill in the missing numbers in this schedule.

STUDENT ID NUMBER	FIRST NAME	LAST NAME	SEX	AGE	COUNTRY	YEARS of ENGLISH STUDY
#80035	Maria	Sanchez	F		Mexico	4
#80036	Ahmed		M	19	Kuwait	2
#80037	Hiromi	Takeda			Japan	
#80038	Pablo		M	22		
#80039	Lim	Quan	M			5
#80040		Sarmiento		20		5

List of Students for English I, Section 001, MWF 8:00–9:15, Spring Semester

Exercise 14

Practice with Confusing Letters

The names of some alphabet letters are confusing because they sound very similar. Listen carefully. In this exercise, you will practice some difficult and confusing letters of the English alphabet. You will hear each letter only one time. Look at the three letters. Circle the correct letter that you hear.

Example: YOU HEAR: "P"

ANSWER: B   V   (P)

1. A   I   E
2. G   Y   J
3. H   S   F
4. I   A   E
5. O   U   W
6. G   Y   J
7. E   A   I
8. Q   U   D
9. B   P   V
10. O   Q   C

11. P   B   V
12. R   L   N
13. S   Z   C
14. V   F   B
15. W   Q   K
16. W   U   Q
17. O   U   V
18. D   T   K
19. E   T   D
20. Z   C   S

Exercise
15

Understanding Simple Lectures: Comparing English Programs

You will hear a short lecture. This lecture is about three different English courses at an English language school. Listen carefully. After you hear the lecture, read the questions below. Choose the correct answer and put a check (✓) on the line.

1. Which program has only two hours each day?
   ___ a. the full-time program
   ___ b. the conversation program
   ___ c. the business English program

2. The biggest program is
   ___ a. the full-time program.
   ___ b. the conversation program.
   ___ c. the business English program.

3. Which program has classes in the morning, in the afternoon, and at night?
   ___ a. the full-time program
   ___ b. the conversation program
   ___ c. the business English program

4. Who is Jan Wells?
   ___ a. a student in the full-time program
   ___ b. a teacher in the night classes
   ___ c. the director of the school

5. When can you take business English classes?
   ___ a. Wednesday afternoon
   ___ b. Thursday night
   ___ c. Friday morning

6. The main purpose of this lecture is to
   ___ a. tell about the different English programs.
   ___ b. explain the difference between day classes and night classes.
   ___ c. talk about why there are not four programs.

7. Students in the full-time program study
   ___ a. reading and conversation.
   ___ b. grammar and reading.
   ___ c. conversation and grammar.

8. How many hours a week is the full-time program?
   ___ a. eight
   ___ b. fifteen
   ___ c. twenty

Exercise 16

Pair Talking

Work in pairs. Student A works from this page, and student B works from page 24. Take turns describing the pictures with a dot; your partner can listen and ask questions to identify the correct picture and place a dot by the correct picture. Student A describes questions 1, 3, and 5, which are on this page. Student B describes questions 2, 4, and 6, which are on page 24.

1.	(tree with two figures)	(tree with three figures, dot)	(tree with three figures)	(tree with four figures)
2.	__ B ✓ v	✓ B ✓ V	__ b ✓ V	✓ b ✓ v
3.	SMITH JONES KIM (dot)	Smith Jones Kim	JONES SMITH KIM	Jones Smith Kim
4.	(two houses)	(two houses)	(two houses)	(two houses)
5.	(classroom, dot at right)	(classroom)	(classroom)	(classroom, dot)
6.	(two boys)	(two boys)	(two boys)	(two boys)

B

1.				

1. (row of four tree pictures with figures)

2.

✓ B	__ B	✓ b	__ b
✓ V	✓ v	✓ v	✓ V

3.

Jones	JONES	Smith	SMITH
Smith	SMITH	Jones	JONES
Kim	KIM	Kim	KIM

4. (row of four house pictures)

5. (row of four classroom pictures — chalkboard with "Homework: 24 + 16", globe, clock, wastebasket, desk)

6. (row of four pictures of two boys)

Exercise
17

Speaking/Discussion: School Uniforms

Practice 17A. Preparation

In some places, students have to wear a uniform to school. In Canada and the United States, most students do not have to wear a uniform to school. However, this situation may be changing. There is a great deal of debate about this issue. (You may want to do a Web search on this topic to learn more about it.)

In your opinion, do you think it is correct that students have to wear a uniform to school? Give at least three reasons to support your opinion.

Opinion: _____

_____

_____

_____

Reason 1: _____

_____

_____

_____

Reason 2: _____

_____

_____

_____

Reason 3: _____

_____

_____

_____

Now write at least one reason to support the opposite opinion:

_____

_____

_____

Practice 17B. Group Speaking/Discussion

Now work with a partner or in a group of three to four students. Take turns discussing your responses to the questions in Practice 17A. In the end, do most of the members of your group support or oppose the idea of wearing school uniforms? What are some of the main reasons for this opinion?

Exercise
18

Rapid Vocabulary Review

From the three answers on the right, circle the one that **best explains, is an example of,** or **combines with** the vocabulary word on the left.

VOCABULARY	ANSWERS		
1. **dislike**	a. like a lot	b. not like	c. like only one
2. **each**	a. sometimes	b. every	c. not expensive
3. **how many**	a. a number	b. a name	c. a place
4. **however**	a. and	b. next	c. but
5. **free**	a. no cost	b. no place	c. no stopping
6. **huge**	a. a coin	b. water	c. a mountain
7. **improve**	a. bad → good	b. great → good	c. easy → difficult
8. **at least 4 pages**	a. 4 pages	b. 3 pages	c. 2 pages
9. **in great _____**	a. section	b. check	c. shape
10. **get to class**	a. arrive in class	b. take a class	c. do well in a class
11. **a great deal**	a. with time	b. of time	c. from time
12. **have to go**	a. 100% chance	b. 50% chance	c. 10% chance
13. **so hungry**	a. not hungry	b. a little hungry	c. very hungry
14. **most**	a. 80%	b. 50%	c. 20%
15. **attend**	a. a meeting	b. a store	c. a flower
16. **confuse**	a. 100% sure	b. sure	c. not sure
17. **lecture**	a. talk/listen	b. read/write	c. cook/eat
18. **spell**	a. numbers	b. items	c. letters
19. **tough**	a. not happy	b. not easy	c. not cold
20. **your opinion**	a. do/make	b. think/believe	c. read/write
21. **a uniform**	a. for work	b. for animals	c. for chairs
22. **similar**	a. cat, cats	b. car, eat	c. student, talk
23. **single**	a. 0	b. 1	c. 2
24. **a list of _____**	a. names	b. water	c. 1:42 P.M.
25. **main**	a. schedule	b. pen and pencil	c. important

MORE VOCABULARY PRACTICE ON THE WEB

Go to the activities for unit 1 at www.press.umich.edu/esl/compsite/ targetinglistening/ and do the five vocabulary exercises there. Record your scores here. The best score in each exercise is 20.

Quiz 1.1. Your Score ——————————— / 20 ———

Quiz 1.2. Your Score ——————————— / 20 ———

Quiz 1.3. Your Score ——————————— / 20 ———

Quiz 1.4. Your Score ——————————— / 20 ———

Quiz 1.5. Your Score ——————————— / 20 ———

UNIT 2

Food

Listening Activity: Understanding Orders in a Restaurant

This listening activity takes place in a restaurant. On the tape, you are going to hear people at two different tables. The server is going to ask each of them what they would like to order. When the customers tell the server their order, put a check mark (✓) by the items that each person orders. The first conversation is for table 1. The next conversation is for table 2.

TABLE 1: The server's name is Ann.

	hamburger	cheeseburger	french fries	soft drink	water	iced tea
1. Michael	○	○	○	○	○	○
2. Emily	○	○	○	○	○	○
3. Sarah	○	○	○	○	○	○
4. Nicholas	○	○	○	○	○	○

TABLE 2: The server's name is Daniel.

	chocolate cake	ice cream	apple pie	coffee	tea
1. Kaitlyn	○	○	○	○	○
2. Brianna	○	○	○	○	○
3. Ashley	○	○	○	○	○
4. Hannah	○	○	○	○	○

Exercise 2

Dictation in a Dialogue: Ordering in a Restaurant

This dialogue is a conversation at a restaurant. The people in the dialogue are the server and two customers.

There are seven blank lines in the dialogue. Fill in each blank line with the correct sentence that you will hear.

Listen carefully. You will hear a number. Find that sentence number. You will hear each sentence three times. First, listen to the sentence. Repeat the sentence. Then listen again. Write the sentence. Finally, listen again. Check your sentence. The number in parentheses is the number of words in the sentence. Now let's begin with number 1.

Susan: Hi, I'm Susan, and I'll be your server tonight. Here are some menus for you. ❶ _____

_____? (7)

Bob: Yes, I'll have a glass of iced tea.

Susan: OK. And what can I get for you?

Karen: ❷ _____? (6)
            (a few minutes later)

Susan: ❸ _____. (4)
            May I take your dinner order now?

Karen: Sure. The roast beef special sounds great. That's what I want.

Susan: ❹ _____. (6)

            ❺ _____? (5)

Karen: Potatoes.

Susan: OK. Roast beef special with potatoes. And for you, sir?

Bob: I'd like the steak dinner.

Susan:	**❻** _____? (7)
Bob:	Medium.
Susan:	That comes with your choice of rice, potatoes, or noodles.
Bob:	**❼** _____ _____? (11)
Susan:	Thank you very much. I'll take your order to the kitchen right now.
Susan, Bob:	Thanks.

Extra Practice. **Listening Practice**

Close your books. Listen to the complete dialogue from Exercise 2. If there is any part that you cannot understand well, listen to that part again. (Try to listen to this dialogue without looking at your book. This is a good way to improve your listening.)

Extra Practice. **Dialogue Practice**

Work in groups of three. Look at Exercise 2 again. Each person will be one of the characters in the dialogue. Read the dialogue as the characters. When you have finished, change characters and read it through one more time. After you have finished, you may want to listen to the recording of the dialogue one more time.

Exercise 3

Understanding Yes-No Questions in a Cooking Class

This listening practice takes place in a cooking class. A chef is explaining how to cook several dishes. The students in the cooking class are asking the chef some questions.

Listen carefully. You will hear ten questions about the dishes. What is the first word of the question? Circle the first word of the question.

Example: YOU HEAR: "Is this dish popular in Mexico?"

            ANSWER: Am   (Is)   Are

1. Am	Is	Are		6. Am	Is	Are
2. Am	Is	Are		7. Am	Is	Are
3. Am	Is	Are		8. Am	Is	Are
4. Am	Is	Are		9. Am	Is	Are
5. Am	Is	Are		10. Am	Is	Are

Exercise

4

Telephone Numbers for Restaurants

In this exercise you will hear telephone numbers for different restaurants. Each number will be repeated for you. Write the number by the name of the restaurant.

Example: YOU HEAR: "The telephone number for Sam's Sandwich Shop is 862-4413."

ANSWER: _____ 862-4413 _____

1. Chan's Chinese Restaurant   _____

2. Mary's Hamburger Place   _____

3. Italian restaurant   _____

4. Pizza Place   _____

5. United Chinese Buffet   _____

6. Nico's Greek Diner   _____

7. Memories of India   _____

8. Gina's on the Bay   _____

9. Parkside Café   _____

10. The Noodle House   _____

Exercise
5

Speaking/Discussion: Tipping in a Restaurant

Practice 5A. Preparation

Read these three questions about restaurant servers and tipping.
Write your answers on the lines provided.

1. When you eat in a restaurant, what percent of the bill do you usually
   leave for a tip? When do you tip more than that? When do you tip
   less?

   _____

   _____

   _____

   _____

   _____

2. Think of a specific time that you did not leave your usual tip. What
   happened that caused you to leave less of a tip?

   _____

   _____

   _____

   _____

   _____

3. Do you think that you could be a server in a restaurant?
   Why or why not?

   _____

   _____

   _____

   _____

   _____

Practice 5B. Group Speaking/Discussion

Now work with a partner or in a group of three to four students. Take turns discussing your responses to the questions in Practice 5A.

Exercise
6

Recognition of the Letters *A* and *E*

Listen carefully. In this exercise, you will hear one letter. You will hear the letter **A** or the letter **E**. Write the letter that you hear. This is a rapid exercise.

Example: YOU HEAR: "A"

   ANSWER: <u>A</u>

1. ___   6. ___   11. ___

2. ___   7. ___   12. ___

3. ___   8. ___   13. ___

4. ___   9. ___   14. ___

5. ___   10. ___   15. ___

Exercise
7

Spelling Words with the Letters _A_ and _E_

In this exercise, you will write the words that you hear. The words will have the letters **A** and **E** in them. Each word will be repeated. Listen carefully.

Example: YOU HEAR: "east. e-a-s-t. east."

ANSWER: _east_

1. _____   6. _____

2. _____   7. _____

3. _____   8. _____

4. _____   9. _____

5. _____   10. _____

Exercise
8

Understanding Simple Conversations: Ordering in a Restaurant

You will hear a short conversation between three people in a restaurant. One is the server, and the other two are customers. Listen carefully. After you hear the conversation, read the questions below. Put a check (✓) by the correct answer.

1. What does Jordan say about the potato salad?
   —— a. that he ate it before
   —— b. that a friend said that it was good
   —— c. that he does not want to eat it today

2. What is Allison's food selection?
   —— a. tuna salad
   —— b. tuna sandwich
   —— c. tuna and spaghetti

3. How many side items does the server tell them about?
   —— a. two
   —— b. three
   —— c. four

4. Which of these three items did Jordan and Allison **not** order?
   —— a. tomato soup
   —— b. potato salad
   —— c. salad

5. Which of these statements is false?
   —— a. Allison ordered first.
   —— b. Allison likes green beans.
   —— c. Allison asked for iced tea.

6. Jordan ordered
   —— a. fried chicken, tomato soup, potato salad, and iced tea.
   —— b. fried chicken, tomato soup, green beans, and iced tea.
   —— c. fried chicken, potato soup, green beans, and iced tea.

SINGULAR and PLURAL

In English, we add the letter **S** to a word when the word is plural (more than one).

1 book, 2 book**s**   1 cat, 3 cat**s**   1 car, 5 car**s**

Exercise
9

Singular and Plural

You will hear a sentence about food. Pay attention to singular and plural. Circle the word that you hear.

Example: YOU HEAR: "Please give me two sandwiches."

                ANSWER: sandwich   (sandwiches)

   1. student   students

   2. cup   cups

   3. week   weeks

   4. lemon   lemons

   5. carrot   carrots

   6. menu   menus

   7. map   maps

   8. cake   cakes

   9. restaurant   restaurants

10. dessert   desserts

Understanding Subject Pronouns

Listen carefully. You will hear a short statement. Select the answer that is similar to the statement that you hear. Circle the letter of the correct answer.

Example: YOU HEAR: "The book is good."

                ANSWER: (a.) It is good.

                            b. They are good.

1. a. They are late.
   b. We are late.

2. a. He is a doctor.
   b. They are doctors.

3. a. It is on the table.
   b. They are on the table.

4. a. She is thirsty.
   b. They are thirsty.

5. a. It is beautiful.
   b. They are beautiful.

6. a. He is a student.
   b. They are students.

7. a. She is nice.
   b. They are nice.

8. a. It is right.
   b. They are right.

9. a. It is green.
   b. They are green.

10. a. She is French.
    b. They are French.

11. a. It is very cold.
    b. They are very cold.

12. a. It is on the table.
    b. They are on the table.

13. a. It is ready now.
    b. They are ready now.

14. a. She works a lot.
    b. They work a lot.

Exercise
11

Affirmative and Negative

Listen carefully. You will hear a statement. If the statement is affirmative, circle the plus sign (+). If the statement is negative, circle the minus sign (–).

Example: YOU HEAR: "They aren't hungry now."

               ANSWER: +   (–)

1.	+ –	9.	+ –	17.	+ –
2.	+ –	10.	+ –	18.	+ –
3.	+ –	11.	+ –	19.	+ –
4.	+ –	12.	+ –	20.	+ –
5.	+ –	13.	+ –	21.	+ –
6.	+ –	14.	+ –	22.	+ –
7.	+ –	15.	+ –	23.	+ –
8.	+ –	16.	+ –	24.	+ –

Speaking/Discussion: Fast Food Restaurants

Practice 12A. Preparation

Fast food restaurants are a part of American life. The most famous fast food restaurant is McDonald's, but there are many others. Read these questions about fast food restaurants. Write your answers on the lines provided.

1. What is your favorite type of fast food? Why?

   _____

   _____

   _____

   _____

   _____

   _____

   _____

2. What makes a fast food restaurant popular or successful? What are the "magic" qualities that can guarantee success?

   _____

   _____

   _____

   _____

   _____

   _____

   _____

3. People have different opinions as to whether or not fast food restaurants are a good thing for a country and its culture. What do you think? Are fast food restaurants good or bad for society at large? Explain your answer.

_____

_____

_____

_____

_____

_____

_____

_____

_____

Practice 12B. Group Speaking/Discussion

Now work with a partner or in a group of three to four students. Take turns discussing your responses to the questions in Practice 12A.

Exercise 13

Same or Different: Understanding Small Differences between Sentences

In this exercise, you will hear two sentences. If they are the same, circle S. If they are different, circle D.

Example: YOU HEAR: "It's hot in here. It's not in here."

ANSWER: S   (D)

1. S D	9. S D	17. S D
2. S D	10. S D	18. S D
3. S D	11. S D	19. S D
4. S D	12. S D	20. S D
5. S D	13. S D	21. S D
6. S D	14. S D	22. S D
7. S D	15. S D	23. S D
8. S D	16. S D	24. S D

Exercise 14

Answering Yes-No Questions with Short Answers

Listen carefully. You will hear a question. Choose the correct answer, and circle the letter of that answer.

Example: YOU HEAR: "Is that book good?"

          ANSWER: (a.) Yes, it is.

                     b. Yes, they are.

                     c. Yes, he is.

1. a. Yes, I am.
   b. Yes, you are.
   c. Yes, they are.

2. a. No, she isn't.
   b. No, it isn't.
   c. No, he isn't.

3. a. Yes, they are.
   b. Yes, we are.
   c. Yes, I am.

4. a. Yes, it is.
   b. Yes, I am.
   c. Yes, we are.

5. a. No, I am not.
   b. No, you aren't.
   c. No, he isn't.

6. a. No, I am not.
   b. No, he isn't.
   c. No, it isn't.

7. a. Yes, we are.
   b. Yes, they are.
   c. Yes, you are.

8. a. Yes, they are.
   b. Yes, it is.
   c. Yes, she is.

9. a. No, we aren't.
   b. No, they aren't.
   c. No, he isn't.

10. a. Yes, they are.
    b. Yes, she is.
    c. Yes, he is.

11. a. Yes, I am.

    b. Yes, it is.

    c. Yes, he is.

12. a. No, he isn't.

    b. No, she isn't.

    c. No, they aren't.

13. a. No, they aren't.

    b. No, you aren't.

    c. No, it isn't.

14. a. Yes, I am.

    b. Yes, you are.

    c. Yes, she is.

Exercise
15

Listening Activity: Recipe for "Big Chocolate Chip Cookies"

Here is a recipe called "Big Chocolate Chip Cookies." These cookies are very popular, and they are very easy to make. In this listening activity, you will find a list of the ingredients followed by a list of the steps in making the cookies. When you see words in parentheses, circle the word(s) that you hear. When you see a blank line, fill in the blank with the word that you hear. A good homework assignment is for you to go home and make these cookies for your class! The first two answers have been done for you.

Recipe for Big Chocolate Chip Cookies

Ingredients:

<u>2</u> cups all-purpose flour

((1 teaspoon,) 2 teaspoons) baking soda

1/2 teaspoon salt

3/4 cup melted _____

1 cup packed brown (sugar, flour)

(1/2, 1, 2) cup white sugar

___ tablespoons vanilla extract

2 (cups, tablespoons) semisweet chocolate (chip, chips)

1 _____

1 egg yolk

Steps:

1. Preheat the oven to 325 (degree, degrees) F (165 degrees C).
2. Put oil or butter on cookie sheets.
3. Mix together the flour, baking soda, and _____.
4. In another (bowl, dish), mix together the melted butter, brown sugar, and white sugar until well blended.
5. Add the vanilla, egg, and _____. Mix until light and creamy.
6. Mix in the dry ingredients with the _____ ingredients until just blended.

7. Add the chocolate chips by _____ using a wooden spoon.

8. Drop cookie mixture 1/4 cup at a time onto the prepared cookie (sheet, sheets). Make sure that the cookies are about (2, 3) inches apart.

9. Bake for ___ to 17 minutes in the preheated oven or until the edges are lightly toasted. Let cookies cool for about ___ minutes before eating.

Exercise 16

Understanding and Unscrambling Letters to Form Words

In this exercise, you will hear a group of letters. Each group of letters will be repeated one time. Write the letters on the line on the left. Then try to move the letters around to make a word. Write the word on the line on the right. Every word in this exercise is the name of a kind of food.

Example: YOU HEAR: "m-a-r-e-c"

ANSWER: _____marec_____   _____cream_____

scrambled letters   name of food

1. _____   _____

2. _____   _____

3. _____   _____

4. _____   _____

5. _____   _____

6. _____   _____

7. _____   _____

8. _____   _____

9. _____   _____

10. _____   _____

Exercise 17

Recognition of Words and Numbers within Short Conversations

In this exercise, you will hear a short conversation between two people. The first person will ask a question, and the second person will answer. Listen carefully to the answer and put a check (✓) by what you hear.

Example: YOU HEAR: "May I help you?"

"Yes, I'd like two oranges and an apple."

ANSWER: ＿ 2 apples

✓ 2 oranges

1. ＿ 2 pens

＿ 2 pencils

2. ＿ 3 dimes

＿ 3 nickels

3. ＿ 2 tomatoes

＿ 2 onions

4. ＿ 1 stamp

＿ 1 postcard

5. ＿ 1 dog

＿ 1 cat

6. ＿ 4 huge windows

＿ 4 glass doors

7. ＿ 3 boys

＿ 3 girls

8. ＿ 6 days

＿ 6 nights

9. ＿ 13 students

＿ 13 teachers

10. ＿ 3 hours

＿ 3 minutes

Exercise
18

Sound Practice: /s/ and /z/

You will hear one word. The word has the sound of either **S** or **Z**.
Write the letter of the sound that you hear on the line.

Beginning	**Middle**	**End**	
1. ___	6. ___	11. ___	16. ___
2. ___	7. ___	12. ___	17. ___
3. ___	8. ___	13. ___	18. ___
4. ___	9. ___	14. ___	19. ___
5. ___	10. ___	15. ___	20. ___

For extra practice, can you think of more examples?

Beginning	**Middle**	**End**
1. _____	4. _____	7. _____
2. _____	5. _____	8. _____
3. _____	6. _____	9. _____

Exercise
19

Sound Practice: /s/ and /z/

Look at the list of words below. You will hear a sentence that has one of these words. Circle the word that you hear.

1. bus

    buzz

2. ice

    eyes

3. hiss

    his

4. price

    prize

5. rice

    rise

6. race

    rays

7. bus

    buzz

8. it's

    is

9. dice

    dies

10. it's

    is

Understanding Simple Lectures: U.S. Food

You will hear a short lecture about food in the United States. This lecture talks about foods found in five different areas of the United States. Listen carefully. After you hear the lecture, read the questions below. Put a check (✓) by the correct answer. Ready? Let's begin.

1. The food that is eaten in Texas is called
   ___ a. Mex-Tex.
   ___ b. Tex-Mex.
   ___ c. Mexican.

2. What is a midnight?
   ___ a. a plate made with rice and beans
   ___ b. a special kind of long bread
   ___ c. a sandwich

3. Black beans are part of the typical food in
   ___ a. Chicago.
   ___ b. New Orleans.
   ___ c. south Florida.

4. Which of these is part of Creole food?
   ___ a. Chinese
   ___ b. Cuban
   ___ c. French

5. Where do people cook jambalaya?
   ___ a. San Francisco
   ___ b. New Orleans
   ___ c. south Florida

6. Sourdough is common in
   ___ a. San Francisco.
   ___ b. New Orleans.
   ___ c. New York.

7. Tamales and enchiladas are typical foods in
   —— a. Louisiana.
   —— b. Florida.
   —— c. Texas.

8. Gumbo is cooked in
   —— a. New York.
   —— b. New Orleans.
   —— c. south Florida.

Exercise 21

Pair Talking

Work in pairs. Student A works from this page, and student B works from page 56. Take turns describing the pictures with a dot; your partner can listen and ask questions to identify the correct picture and place a dot by the correct picture. Student A describes questions 1, 3, and 5, which are on this page. Student B describes questions 2, 4, and 6, which are on page 56.

A

1.			ice ice	eyes eyes
2.				
3.				
4.				
5.	A e a	a E A	E e a	e E A
6.	$ 13	$ 30	$ 13	$ 30

B

1.			**eyes** **eyes**	**ice** **ice**
2.				
3.				
4.				
5.	E e a	e E A	A e a	a E A
6.	$ 13	$ 30	$ 13	$ 30

Exercise 22

Speaking/Discussion: Talking about Your Favorite Dish

Practice 22A. Preparation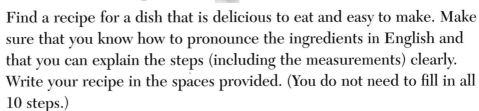

Find a recipe for a dish that is delicious to eat and easy to make. Make sure that you know how to pronounce the ingredients in English and that you can explain the steps (including the measurements) clearly. Write your recipe in the spaces provided. (You do not need to fill in all 10 steps.)

Recipe Name: _____

Ingredients: _____

_____

_____

_____

_____

_____

_____

_____

_____

Steps:

1. _____

_____

_____

2. _____

_____

_____

3. _____

_____

_____

4. _____

_____

_____

5. _____

_____

_____

6. _____

_____

_____

7. _____

_____

_____

8. _____

_____

_____

9. _____

_____

_____

10. _____

_____

_____

Practice 22B. Group Speaking/Discussion

Now work with a partner or in a group of two to four students. Take turns presenting your recipes in Practice 22A. As each speaker explains the steps, try to visualize yourself making the dish. If you do not understand how to pronounce the name of an ingredient or how to do one of the steps, ask the speaker for clarification.

Exercise
23

Rapid Vocabulary Review

From the three answers on the right, circle the one that **best explains, is an example of,** or **combines with** the vocabulary word on the left.

VOCABULARY		ANSWERS	
1. **bay**	a. cabbage	b. water	c. air
2. **a bowl of ___**	a. drop	b. early	c. soup
3. **cookies**	a. sweet	b. clean	c. shy
4. **I'm on a ___.**	a. degree	b. diet	c. dessert
5. **lettuce**	a. vegetable	b. influence	c. successful
6. **flour**	a. wheat	b. heavy	c. percent
7. **guarantee**	a. harmful	b. 100% sure	c. go ahead
8. **melt**	a. ice → water	b. water → air	c. air → humans
9. **mixture**	a. not yet	b. lightly	c. together
10. **pets**	a. animal	b. peach	c. stamp
11. **___ meat**	a. recipe	b. rare	c. oven
12. **I don't think ___**	a. and	b. but	c. so
13. **___ a few minutes**	a. before	b. next	c. in
14. **There ___ 2 cars.**	a. park	b. customers	c. are
15. **tip**	a. money	b. animal	c. steps
16. **tuna**	a. fish	b. vanilla	c. toast
17. **turn on**	a. the table	b. the window	c. the TV
18. **vacation**	a. trip	b. push	c. chef
19. **wash**	a. way	b. water	c. wood
20. **wonderful**	a. +	b. 0	c. −
21. **would like**	a. speak	b. want	c. cost
22. **yolk**	a. year	b. egg	c. wheat
23. **enjoy**	a. take	b. like	c. wake
24. **envelope**	a. a letter	b. a book	c. an egg
25. **fresh ___**	a. several	b. seafood	c. snore

MORE VOCABULARY PRACTICE ON THE WEB

Go to the activities for unit 2 at www.press.umich.edu/esl/compsite/ targetinglistening/ and do the five vocabulary exercises there. Record your scores here. The best score in each exercise is 20.

Quiz 2.1. Your Score _____ / 20 _____

Quiz 2.2. Your Score _____ / 20 _____

Quiz 2.3. Your Score _____ / 20 _____

Quiz 2.4. Your Score _____ / 20 _____

Quiz 2.5. Your Score _____ / 20 _____

Animals and Pets

Listening Activity: Taking a Test about Cats

How well do you know cats, compared to humans and dogs? Here is a quick test about cats. Listen to the questions and then choose what you think the correct answers are.

The questions are not written out on the page, so listen carefully. Each question will be read two times.

A Pet Test: A Test about Cats

Question 1.   — cats   — dogs

Question 2.   — 24   — 28   — 30   — 32   — 36

Question 3.   — 24   — 28   — 30   — 32   — 42

Question 4.   — 24   — 28   — 30   — 32   — 36

Question 5.   — 20   — 40   — 60   — 80   — 100

Question 6.   — 104   — 164   — 206   — 230

Question 7.   — 140   — 190   — 240   — 290

Question 8.   — 16   — 18   — 20   — 24

Question 9.   _____

Question 10. _____

Question 11. _____

Question 12. _____

EXTRA SPEAKING PRACTICE: Before you find out the correct answers, compare your answers with a partner. How many answers are the same? Which ones are different?

Exercise 2

Dictation in a Dialogue: Taking Your Pet to the Vet (veterinarian)

This dialogue is a conversation about pets. The people in the dialogue are two friends who are talking about their pets.

There are seven blank lines in the dialogue. Fill in each blank line with the correct sentence that you will hear.

Listen carefully. You will hear a number. Find that sentence number. You will hear each sentence three times. First, listen to the sentence. Repeat the sentence. Then listen again. Write the sentence. Finally, listen again. Check your sentence. The number in parentheses is the number of words in the sentence. Now let's begin with number 1.

Mark: Hi, Anna. How are you?

Anna: Just fine. Wow, I haven't seen you in a long time. What are you doing today?

Mark: ❶ _____? (10) Would you like to go?

Anna: I can't. I'd love to go, but I can't. ❷ _____

_____? (9)

Mark: Oh, really? Why? ❸ _____? (3)

Anna: I'm not sure. ❹ _____? (6)

Mark: I'm sorry to hear that. Where is your vet's office?

Anna: I go to Dr. Samuel. Her office is on Lincoln

Road. ❺ _____? (4)

Mark: Yes, I do.

Anna: ❻ _____? (7)

Mark: Yes, it is. I like Dr. Samuel. She has a really good way of explaining things. I like how her office treats my dog.

❼ _____

_____? (8)

Anna: Exactly. If my cat has any problems, I always take her to Dr. Samuel.

Extra Practice. **Listening Practice**

Close your books. Listen to the complete dialogue from Exercise 2. If there is any part that you cannot understand well, listen to that part again. (Try to listen to this dialogue without looking at your book. This is a good way to improve your listening.)

Extra Practice. **Dialogue Practice**

Work in pairs. Look at Exercise 2 again. Each person will be one of the characters in the dialogue. Read the dialogue as the characters. When you have finished, change characters and read it again. After you have finished, you may want to listen to the recording of the dialogue one more time.

Exercise
3

Understanding Questions in a Pet Store

This listening practice takes place in a pet store. The pet store owner is explaining some things about pets. Some customers are asking questions.

Listen carefully. You will hear ten questions about pets. What is the first word of the question? Circle the first word of the question.

Example: YOU HEAR: "Do you have a pet?"

ANSWER: (Do)   Does

1. Do   Does   6. Do   Does

2. Do   Does   7. Do   Does

3. Do   Does   8. Do   Does

4. Do   Does   9. Do   Does

5. Do   Does   10. Do   Does

Speaking/Discussion: Talking about Your Pets

Practice 4A. Preparation

Read these three questions about pets. Write your answers to the questions on the lines provided.

1. (a) Have you ever owned a pet? ———
       If yes, do (b), (c), and (e) only.
       If not, do (d) and (e) only.

   (b) If yes, what kind of pet was it? ————————————

       Where did you get the pet? ————————————

       How long did you have the pet? ————————————

   (c) What were some things you liked most about your pet?

       ————————————————————————————————

       ————————————————————————————————

   (d) Give an important reason why you have never owned a pet.

       ————————————————————————————————

       ————————————————————————————————

   (e) What are three positive and three negative things about owning a pet?

       Positives:

       ————————————————————————————————

       ————————————————————————————————

       ————————————————————————————————

       Negatives:

       ————————————————————————————————

       ————————————————————————————————

       ————————————————————————————————

2. If you could have any pet, what would it be and why?

_____

_____

_____

3. Some people treat their pets as if they are people. Can you give an example of this?

_____

_____

_____

How do you feel about this? _____

_____

_____

_____

Practice 4B. Group Speaking/Discussion

Now work with a partner or in a group of three to four students. Take turns discussing your responses to the questions in Practice 4A.

Numbers (21–100)		
21 twenty-one	51 fifty-one	81 eighty-one
22 twenty-two	52 fifty-two	82 eighty-two
23 twenty-three	53 fifty-three	83 eighty-three
24 twenty-four	54 fifty-four	84 eighty-four
25 twenty-five	55 fifty-five	85 eighty-five
26 twenty-six	56 fifty-six	86 eighty-six
27 twenty-seven	57 fifty-seven	87 eighty-seven
28 twenty-eight	58 fifty-eight	88 eighty-eight
29 twenty-nine	59 fifty-nine	89 eighty-nine
30 thirty	60 sixty	90 ninety
31 thirty-one	61 sixty-one	91 ninety-one
32 thirty-two	62 sixty-two	92 ninety-two
33 thirty-three	63 sixty-three	93 ninety-three
34 thirty-four	64 sixty-four	94 ninety-four
35 thirty-five	65 sixty-five	95 ninety-five
36 thirty-six	66 sixty-six	96 ninety-six
37 thirty-seven	67 sixty-seven	97 ninety-seven
38 thirty-eight	68 sixty-eight	98 ninety-eight
39 thirty-nine	69 sixty-nine	99 ninety-nine
40 forty	70 seventy	100 one hundred
41 forty-one	71 seventy-one	
42 forty-two	72 seventy-two	
43 forty-three	73 seventy-three	
44 forty-four	74 seventy-four	
45 forty-five	75 seventy-five	
46 forty-six	76 seventy-six	
47 forty-seven	77 seventy-seven	
48 forty-eight	78 seventy-eight	
49 forty-nine	79 seventy-nine	
50 fifty	80 eighty	

Recognition of Numbers 21–100

In this exercise, you will hear one number. Find the number and put a circle around the correct answer.

Example: YOU HEAR: "twenty-eight"

ANSWER: (28)   61   39

1.	82	94	36	11.	92	27	40
2.	62	97	27	12.	21	50	38
3.	74	39	28	13.	43	82	90
4.	63	71	23	14.	89	22	36
5.	72	28	53	15.	71	51	31
6.	26	28	21	16.	72	41	93
7.	77	52	31	17.	93	43	63
8.	79	30	49	18.	54	72	89
9.	62	29	55	19.	40	80	60
10.	44	21	100	20.	32	68	22

Exercise 6

Recognition of Numbers 21–100

Listen carefully. You will hear a number from 21 to 100. Write the number in numeral form that you hear. Each number will be repeated.

Example: YOU HEAR: "eighty-four"

ANSWER: <u>84</u>

1. _____   11. _____

2. _____   12. _____

3. _____   13. _____

4. _____   14. _____

5. _____   15. _____

6. _____   16. _____

7. _____   17. _____

8. _____   18. _____

9. _____   19. _____

10. _____   20. _____

Exercise 7

Understanding Simple Conversations: Getting a Puppy

You will hear a short conversation between Marilyn and Bob. In this conversation, Marilyn is thinking of buying a puppy from Bob. Listen carefully. After you hear the conversation, read the questions below. Put a check (✓) by the correct answer.

1. What is the name of the new owner of the puppy?
   ___ a. Bob
   ___ b. Linda
   ___ c. Marilyn

2. Marilyn wanted to
   ___ a. meet Bob for lunch.
   ___ b. hold the brown puppy.
   ___ c. hold the white puppy.

3. Marilyn's apartment is
   ___ a. one bedroom.
   ___ b. two bedrooms.
   ___ c. too small.

4. Bob asked Marilyn what time she got home from work. She said
   ___ a. around three o'clock.
   ___ b. around five o'clock.
   ___ c. at 4:30.

5. How much did the puppy cost?
   ___ a. $25
   ___ b. free (no cost)
   ___ c. $35

Recognition of the Letters *E* and *I*

For many English learners, the letters **E** and **I** are confusing. Listen carefully. In this exercise, you will hear one letter. You will hear the letter **E** or the letter **I**. Write the letter that you hear. This is a rapid exercise.

Example: YOU HEAR: "I"

              ANSWER: ___I___

1. ___   6. ___   11. ___

2. ___   7. ___   12. ___

3. ___   8. ___   13. ___

4. ___   9. ___   14. ___

5. ___   10. ___   15. ___

**Exercise
9**

Spelling Words with the Letters *E* and *I*

For many English learners, the letters **E** and **I** are confusing. Listen carefully. You will hear one word. Write the word on the line. The letters will be repeated.

Example: YOU HEAR: "n-i-c-e"

ANSWER: ___nice___

1. _____ 6. _____

2. _____ 7. _____

3. _____ 8. _____

4. _____ 9. _____

5. _____ 10. _____

Exercise 10

Speaking/Discussion: Lost Pets, Found Pets

Practice 10A. Preparation

People love their pets. When their pets are lost, people obviously worry a great deal until they find their pets again.

When people lose their pets, they put announcements in newspapers or post notices at a nearby supermarket or pet store that has a public notice board. Here are two announcements. The first is from someone who has lost an animal. The second is from someone who has found an animal.

Lost Pet!

Pet cat named Tuxedo. 1-year-old male cat, black and white, white whiskers, wearing a green collar with bell. Weighs approximately 10 pounds. Shy at first but very friendly cat. Last seen near Hudson Elementary School area. Call (477) 555-4581. Reward $100.

Found Pet!

Small female Chihuahua. Light brown. Very friendly but can be noisy when frightened. Call (281) 555-6261 between 6 p.m. and 9 p.m. weekdays.

Imagine that you have lost your pet. Write a lost pet announcement. (If you wish, you may pretend that you have found a pet and write a found pet announcement.)

Now work in small groups. Take turns presenting your pet announcements. Are there any similarities in your announcements? Are there things that are not clear? Can you discuss how to improve them?

Exercise
11

Statement (.) or Question (?)

Listen carefully. If you hear a statement, circle the period. If you hear a question, circle the question mark.

Example: YOU HEAR: "Does John have a dog?"

                   ANSWER: .   ⟨?⟩

1. . ?	6. . ?
2. . ?	7. . ?
3. . ?	8. . ?
4. . ?	9. . ?
5. . ?	10. . ?

Listening Activity: A Pet Store Owner's Recommendation

Bob is going to the pet shop to buy a new pet. He is not sure which kind of pet to buy. Listen to what Bob says about himself. Circle the correct description of Bob in numbers 1 through 4. Then listen to what the pet store owner says about each pet. The pet store owner will make a recommendation for Bob. In number 5, circle the pet store owner's recommendation.

1. Bob lives in a   Bob lives in a
   large apartment.   small apartment.

2. Bob works   Bob works
   long hours.   short hours.

3. Bob likes   Bob likes
   soft music.   loud music.

4. Bob is scared   Bob is scared
   of spiders.   of snakes.

5. Circle the pet that the store owner says is a good pet for Bob.

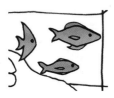  

Exercise 13

Affirmative/Negative

Listen carefully. You will hear a statement. If the statement is affirmative, circle the plus sign (+). If the statement is negative, circle the minus sign (−).

Example: YOU HEAR: "Mike enjoys reading about animals."

ANSWER: -

1. + −	6. + −	11. + −
2. + −	7. + −	12. + −
3. + −	8. + −	13. + −
4. + −	9. + −	14. + −
5. + −	10. + −	15. + −

Exercise 14

Answering Yes-No Questions with Short Answers

Listen carefully. You will hear a question. Choose the correct answer, and circle the letter of that answer.

Example: YOU HEAR: "Does Jonathan like cats?"

ANSWER: a. Yes, he did.

(b.) Yes, he does.

c. Yes, they do.

1. a. Yes, it does.
   b. No, we don't.
   c. Yes, they do.

2. a. No, it doesn't.
   b. No, they don't.
   c. No, he doesn't.

3. a. Yes, they do.
   b. Yes, you do.
   c. Yes, it does.

4. a. No, they don't.
   b. No, it doesn't.
   c. No, we don't.

5. a. Yes, they do.
   b. Yes, you do.
   c. Yes, he does.

6. a. Yes, she does.
   b. Yes, I do.
   c. Yes, they do.

7. a. Yes, we do.
   b. Yes, they do.
   c. Yes, it does.

8. a. No, he doesn't.
   b. No, they don't.
   c. No, it doesn't.

9. a. Yes, she does.
   b. Yes, I do.
   c. Yes, they do.

10. a. No, it doesn't.
    b. No, they don't.
    c. No, he doesn't.

Pronunciation: The Letter S

You know some words that begin with the letter **S**. Some examples are: **s**ome, **s**ix, and **s**peak. Write some more words that begin with the letter **S**: _____ , _____ , and _____ .

The letter S at the **beginning** of a word is like the **S** in **s**ome, **s**ix, and **s**peak. The letter **S** at the **end** of a word is sometimes very different.

The letter **S** can be at the end of a noun. This means plural. For example, 1 book becomes 2 book**s**. The letter **S** can also come at the end of a verb. For example, I take, she take**s**. Whether the **S** is for a plural noun or for the third person singular (**He, She, It**) form of a verb, the pronunciation still follows the same rules.

There are three different ways to pronounce the letter **S** at the end of a word. Sometimes the letter **S** is like the **S** in **s**ome, **s**ix, and **s**peak, but sometimes it is like the letter **Z** in the words **z**oo and **z**ero.

Like **S**	Like **Z**
1 cat	1 bed
2 cat**s**	2 bed**s**
1 cake	1 day
4 cake**s**	4 day**s**
I eat	I need
He eat**s**	He need**s**
We speak	We give
She speak**s**	She give**s**

The **last sound** in the word is important. It is very important to know the sound before the letter **S**.

Sound Practice: *S/Z*

Now read these sentences carefully. Look at the boldfaced words.
Write the last sound before the letter **S**. Then write the pronunciation.
Follow the examples.

	Last Sound	Pronunciation of Letter **S**
1. I like **cakes**.	k	s
2. There are five **vowels**.	l	z
3. There are twenty-six **letters**.	—	—
4. We have two **maps**.	—	—
5. She **plays** well.	—	—
6. I have two **hands**.	—	—
7. He **speaks** French.	—	—
8. I'm in the United **States**.	—	—
9. He **sees** me.	—	—
10. She never **comes** late.	—	—
11. John **goes** home at noon.	—	—
12. She **counts** slowly.	—	—
13. He has three **dogs**.	—	—
14. I usually drink two **cups**.	—	—
15. They have two **radios**.	—	—

Look at your answers very carefully. Do you know the rule now? Do you
know when you will pronounce **S** and when you will pronounce **Z**?

Now we will look at the third pronunciation of the letter **S.** It is different from the first and second pronunciations.

There is a third way to pronounce the letter **S.** When a word ends in the sound of /s/, /z/, /ch/, /sh/, or /j/, you must pronounce a **new syllable.**

A syllable is the sound of a vowel. We can say that syllables are the parts of a word. For example, *write* has only one syllable, *repeat* has two syllables, *United* has three syllables, and *pronunciation* has five syllables. Look:

write	write	1 syllable
repeat	re·peat	2 syllables
united	u·nit·ed	3 syllables
pronunciation	pro·nun·ci·a·tion	5 syllables

In the third pronunciation of **S**, you will pronounce an extra syllable. For example, I watch TV and he watches TV. I practice my pronunciation, and he practices his pronunciation.

<u>Extra syllable</u>

1 kiss
2 kisses

1 bridge
3 bridges

I watch
He watches

I kiss
He kisses

Now do you know the rule for the pronunciation of the letter **S?**

Rule for the pronunciation of **S**

Pronounce:		When the word ends in these sounds:		
GROUP 1 /s/		/f/	laugh	laughs
		/k/	clock	clocks
		/p/	lip	lips
		/t/	cat	cats
		/th/	Ruth	Ruth's
GROUP 2 /z/		/b/	rob	robs
		/d/	bed	beds
		/g/	dog	dogs
		/l/	pencil	pencils
		/m/	name	names
		/r/	car	cars
		/v/	live	lives
	All	/ay/	play	plays
	Vowels	/ee/	see	sees
		/oe/	snow	snows
		/oy/	boy	boys
		/ie/	cry	cries
GROUP 3 /iz/	Extra	/s/	kiss	kisses
	Syllable	/z/	close	closes
		/ch/	watch	watches
		/sh/	wash	washes
		/j/	bridge	bridges

Exercise 16

Pronunciation of the Letter *S*

In this exercise, there is a list of words that end with the letter **S**. Read each word and pronounce it carefully. Put an X in the correct box to show the pronunciation of the letter **S**. Follow the examples.

	/s/	/z/	/iz/		/s/	/z/	/iz/
1. walks	X			17. arrives			
2. watches			X	18. churches			
3. students				19. kisses			
4. speaks				20. lives			
5. bridges				21. sings			
6. numbers				22. is			
7. cars				23. stands			
8. practices				24. lips			
9. washes				25. loves			
10. judges				26. languages			
11. calls				27. telephones			
12. books				28. teaches			
13. likes				29. leaves			
14. dollars				30. taxes			
15. clocks				31. closes			
16. kittens				32. pages			

Exercise
17

Short Conversations: Details

You will hear a short conversation between a man and an operator. The man is calling the operator because he wants to know the telephone number of a place of business. Listen carefully. Put an X by the place that he wants to call and by the correct phone number.

Example: YOU HEAR: "Operator, may I help you?"

"Yes, please. I need the number of the Hamburger Shop."

"Yes, sir. That number is 431-8246."

ANSWER: ___ Table Restaurant

_X_ Hamburger Shop

_X_ 431-8246

___ 431-2846

1. ___ Mary's Clothing Store   ___ 243-8168

   ___ Mary's Baby Store   ___ 243-8618

2. ___ Telephone Company   ___ 456-2011

   ___ Telephone Store   ___ 456-0211

3. ___ Big Library   ___ 467-5089

   ___ Big Bookstore   ___ 467-5098

4. ___ Hungry Fish   ___ 266-4214

   ___ Angry Fish   ___ 266-4124

5. ___ Brown Travel   ___ 663-8129

   ___ Business Travel   ___ 636-8129

6. ___ Sun Bank   ___ 813-4420

   ___ South Bank   ___ 831-4420

7. ___ Table for Two   ___ 618-9262

   ___ Two Tables   ___ 618-2926

8. ___ Watch Repair Shop ___ 492-8879

   ___ Wash a Pair   ___ 492-8897

9. ___ Tennis Shop   ___ 826-6680

   ___ Tennis Shoe Shop ___ 286-6680

10. ___ Glass House   ___ 884-9201

    ___ Grass House   ___ 884-9210

Exercise 18

Understanding Simple Lectures: Vacations and Wild Animals

You will hear a short lecture. This lecture is about an average day during Daniel's summer vacation in the mountains. Listen carefully. After you hear the lecture, read the questions below. Put a check (✓) by the correct answer.

1. Where are the mountains?
   ___ a. in New York State
   ___ b. in New Jersey State
   ___ c. in Colorado State

2. What activity did Daniel do every morning?
   ___ a. buy Italian food
   ___ b. go for a walk
   ___ c. eat strawberries

3. Daniel misses
   ___ a. his fishing time
   ___ b. his delicious sandwiches
   ___ c. the quiet mountains

4. What time of the day did Daniel see a bear?
   ___ a. in the morning
   ___ b. in the afternoon
   ___ c. in the evening

5. The main reason Daniel likes these mountains is that
   ___ a. they are peaceful.
   ___ b. they are a good location for fishing.
   ___ c. he can see many animals.

Exercise
19

Pair Talking

Work in pairs. Student A works from this page, and student B works from page 88. Take turns describing the pictures with a dot; your partner can listen and ask questions to identify the correct picture and place a dot by the correct picture. Student A describes questions 1, 3, and 5, which are on this page. Student B describes questions 2, 4, and 6, which are on page 88.

A

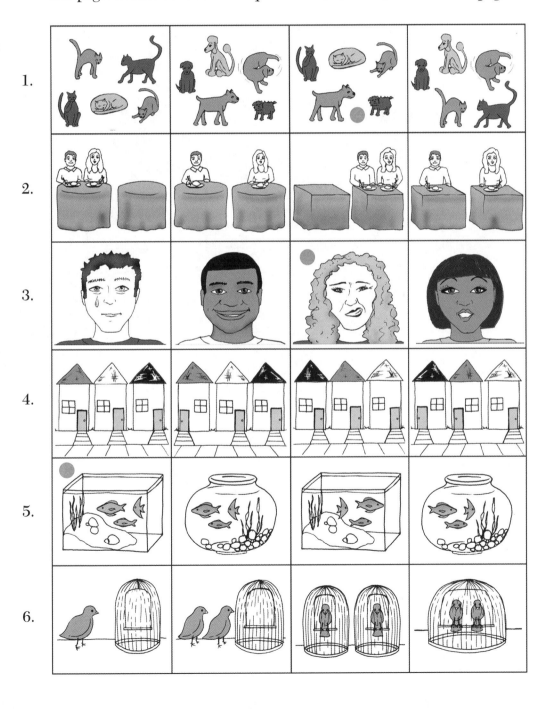

B

1.

2.

3.

4.

5.

6.

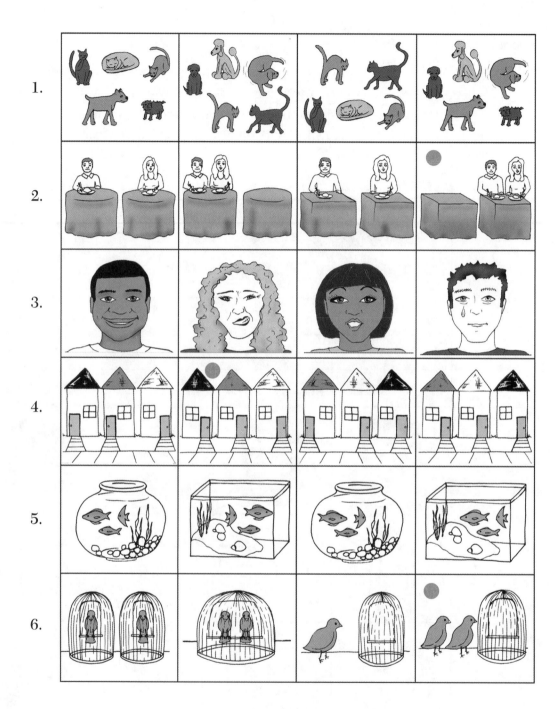

Exercise 20

Speaking/Discussion: Pet Selection

Practice 20A. Preparation

Imagine that you are going to buy a pet at the pet store. The pet store has a good variety of pets in it.

Jack's Pet Store

large dog (40 pounds)	small Chihuahua	green parakeet
adult cat	small puppy	small kitten
a talking bird	goldfish	tropical fish
a large snake	a turtle	a hamster

a. What do you think is the easiest pet to own? What do you think is the most difficult pet to own? Explain your answers.

_____

_____

_____

_____

_____

b. Choose two unusual pets. What food do they eat? How much does the food cost?

_____

_____

_____

_____

_____

c. Which of the pets in this store are suitable for a six-year-old child? Which are not suitable for this child? Why?

_____

_____

_____

_____

_____

d. Which two of the pets in this store are pets that you would not want to have? Why?

_____

_____

_____

_____

_____

Practice 20B. Group Speaking/Discussion

Now work with a partner or in a small group of three to four students. Take turns discussing your responses to the questions in Practice 20A.

Exercise 21

Rapid Vocabulary Review

From the three answers on the right, circle the one that **best explains, is an example of,** or **combines with** the vocabulary word on the left.

VOCABULARY	ANSWERS		
1. **announce**	a. a message	b. a person	c. a telephone
2. **approximately 50**	a. 45–55	b. exactly 50	c. more than 50
3. **bark**	a. a dog	b. a cat	c. a bear
4. **blueberry**	a. meat	b. fruit	c. vegetable
5. **79 is close to ___**	a. 179	b. 79 – 79 = 0	c. 80
6. **cost**	a. $$$	b. ABC	c. ; , ?
7. **the fall**	a. hot weather	b. yellow leaves	c. short pants
8. **female**	a. boy	b. baby	c. girl
9. **finish**	a. end	b. take	c. say
10. **fly**	a. parrot	b. fox	c. turtle
11. **get up**	a. morning	b. afternoon	c. night
12. **imagine**	a. enough	b. pretend	c. take
13. **large**	a. long	b. suitable	c. big
14. **not light**	a. a little quiet	b. weigh a lot	c. a big ceiling
15. **loud**	a. piece	b. noise	c. toenail
16. **negative**	a. +	b. + or –	c. –
17. **special**	a. unusual	b. scared	c. repair
18. **vet**	a. teacher	b. doctor	c. announcer
19. **yard**	a. outside	b. variety	c. obvious
20. **in a long ___**	a. way	b. spider	c. time
21. **variety**	a. type or kind	b. smell or taste	c. food or drink
22. **bread ingredient**	a. meat and fish	b. tomato and lettuce	c. oil and salt
23. **bridge**	a. for a river	b. for a mountain	c. for a judge
24. **snow**	a. blue	b. red	c. white
25. **ears**	a. 2	b. 12	c. 20

MORE VOCABULARY PRACTICE ON THE WEB

Go to the activities for unit 3 at www.press.umich.edu/esl/compsite/
targetinglistening/ and do the five vocabulary exercises there. Record
your scores here. The best score in each exercise is 20.

Quiz 3.1. Your Score ——————————— / 20 ————

Quiz 3.2. Your Score ——————————— / 20 ————

Quiz 3.3. Your Score ——————————— / 20 ————

Quiz 3.4. Your Score ——————————— / 20 ————

Quiz 3.5. Your Score ——————————— / 20 ————

Unit 4

Free Time and Hobbies

Listening Activity: Matching People with Their Hobbies

Many people collect things for their hobby. For example, some people collect things like coins and stamps. However, some people collect unique things.

People will talk about their hobby of collecting different things. Draw a line from the person's name on the left to the name of the thing that he or she collects on the right. (One name and one thing will not be used.)

People who collect things	Things that people collect
David	old photographs
Matthew	matchbooks
Jordan	cookie jars
Nicholas	football programs
Jasmine	baseball cards
Samantha	postcards
Emily	stamps
Joshua	toasters
Elizabeth	old movie posters
Katherine	cooking program videos
Keith	international cookbooks

EXTRA SPEAKING PRACTICE: Before you find out the correct answers, compare your answers with a partner. How many answers are the same? Which ones are different?

Exercise
2

Dictation in a Dialogue: Talking about Stamp Collections

This is a dialogue about collecting stamps. The people in the dialogue are two stamp collectors. They are talking about their stamp collections.

There are seven blank lines in the dialogue. Fill in the blank lines with the correct sentences that you will hear.

Listen carefully. You will hear a number. Find that sentence number. You will hear each sentence three times. First, listen to the sentence. Repeat the sentence. Then listen again. Write the sentence. Finally, listen again. Check your sentence. The number in the parentheses is the number of words in the sentence.

David: Jasmine, have you seen my bird stamp from Mongolia?

Jasmine: No, I haven't. Which one is it?

David: ❶ _____ (8)

Jasmine: Oh, I see it now. David, where did you get it?

David: ❷ _____ (6)

Jasmine: Oh, did he go there on vacation?

David: ❸ _____ (8)
              Do you have any stamps from Asia?

Jasmine: ❹ _____ (9)

David: How much is the stamp?

Jasmine: ❺ _____
              _____ (11)
              Do people in Japan still use that stamp?

David: I am not sure, but I have six 50-yen stamps from Japan, too.
              Do you want one?

Jasmine: ❻ _____ (8)

David: No problem. I have six of them.

Jasmine: Where did you get six Japanese stamps?

David: ❼ _____ (9)

Jasmine: What a great friend!

Extra Practice. **Listening Practice**

Close your books. Listen to the complete dialogue from Exercise 2. If there is any part that you cannot understand well, listen to that part again. (Try to listen to this dialogue without looking at your book. This is a good way to improve your listening.)

Extra Practice. **Dialogue Practice**

Work in pairs. Look at Exercise 2 again. Each person will be one of the characters in the dialogue. Read the dialogue as the characters. When you have finished, change characters and read it again. After you have finished, you may want to listen to the recording of the dialogue one more time.

Exercise
3

Understanding Yes-No Questions about Hobbies

You will hear twelve questions about people's hobbies. Listen carefully. Circle the word Do, Does, or Did that you hear in the question.

Example: YOU HEAR: "Do you like to play sports?"

ANSWER: (Do)   Does   Did

1.	Do	Does	Did	7.	Do	Does	Did
2.	Do	Does	Did	8.	Do	Does	Did
3.	Do	Does	Did	9.	Do	Does	Did
4.	Do	Does	Did	10.	Do	Does	Did
5.	Do	Does	Did	11.	Do	Does	Did
6.	Do	Does	Did	12.	Do	Does	Did

Exercise 4

Telephone Numbers: Getting to the Gym

Working out at a gym is a common hobby. In this exercise, two people talk about working out at a gym. In the conversation, one of the people will say a phone number. Write it on the line. Listen carefully. The numbers will **not** be repeated.

1. _____

2. _____

3. _____

4. _____

5. _____

6. _____

7. _____

8. _____

9. _____

10. _____

Exercise
5

Speaking/Discussion: Talking about Your Own Hobby

Practice 5A. Preparation

Everyone has a hobby. (A hobby is something you like to do when you have free time.) Read these five questions about hobbies. Then write your answers to the questions on the lines provided.

1. What is your favorite hobby? _____

2. When did you become interested in this hobby? _____

_____

3. How did you become interested in this hobby? _____

_____

_____

_____

4. Why do you like this hobby? _____

_____

_____

_____

5. What is the best thing about this hobby? _____

_____

_____

_____

_____

_____

Practice 5B. Group Speaking/Discussion

Now work with a partner or in a group of three to four students. Take turns discussing your responses to the questions in Practice 5A. Your goal is to convince the others in your group to take up your hobby.

Exercise
6

Recognition of the Letters *A / E / I*

For many language learners, the letters **A, E,** and **I** are confusing. Listen carefully. In this exercise, you will hear one letter. You will hear the letter **A,** the letter **E,** or the letter **I.** Write the letter on the line. This is a very rapid exercise.

Example: YOU HEAR: "E"

ANSWER: <u>E</u>

1. —   11. —

2. —   12. —

3. —   13. —

4. —   14. —

5. —   15. —

6. —   16. —

7. —   17. —

8. —   18. —

9. —   19. —

10. —   20. —

Exercise
7

Understanding Simple Conversations: Free Time Plans

You will hear a short conversation between Sarah and Kim. In this conversation, Sarah is telling Kim about her plans. Listen carefully.

After you hear the conversation, read the questions below. Choose the correct answer and put a check (✓) on the line.

1. What is Sarah doing on Saturday?
   ___ a. going to a coin collectors' show
   ___ b. going to a Tom Cruise movie
   ___ c. going to dinner with her cousin

2. Sarah has coins from
   ___ a. 50 countries.
   ___ b. 15 countries.
   ___ c. Japan and China.

3. Kim asked what time the show
   ___ a. begins.
   ___ b. is beginning.
   ___ c. finishes.

4. Why does Kim ask her that question?
   ___ a. because her friend is visiting
   ___ b. because her cousin is visiting
   ___ c. because her parents are visiting

5. What time does Kim's visitor arrive at her house?
   ___ a. 5 P.M.
   ___ b. 7 P.M.
   ___ c. 10 P.M.

Travel Hobby: Spelling of Country Names

Travel is a popular hobby for many people. In this exercise, the speaker talks about her experiences with travel. She will say a sentence about traveling to a country. Then she will spell the name of a country. Write the name of the country that you hear.

1. My favorite country is ——————.

2. My favorite city is Oslo. Oslo is located in ——————.

3. In 1990, I visited Dakar. Dakar is a big city in the country of ——————.

4. My first international trip was to ——————.

5. Next year I want to travel to ——————. It is between Norway and Finland.

6. —————— is a special place to visit. This country is next to Thailand.

7. —————— is in Africa. It is located south of Libya.

8. Vienna is the capital of ——————. It is an incredibly beautiful country.

9. —————— is in South America. I visited this country last year.

10. I bought some beautiful carpets in ——————.

Exercise
9

Affirmative vs. Negative: *do, does, did* in Fun Hobby Statements

Listen carefully. You will hear some statements about people's hobbies. If the statement is affirmative, circle the plus sign (+). If the statement is negative, circle the negative sign (−).

Example: YOU HEAR: "Ten years ago, I didn't have any fun hobbies."

ANSWER: +   ⊖

1. + −   7. + −

2. + −   8. + −

3. + −   9. + −

4. + −   10. + −

5. + −   11. + −

6. + −   12. + −

Exercise
10

Speaking/Discussion: Survey of Favorite Pastimes

Practice 10A. Preparation

Read these statements about activities. If you had some free time now, which of these activities sound good to you? Which do not? Circle ① if you do not like to do this activity, ② if you like this activity but not so much, ③ if you enjoy this activity, or ④ if you really enjoy this activity. On the line, explain why you marked 1, 2, 3, or 4. (If you haven't done the activity before, make a guess as to whether you think you'd like it.)

a.   1 2 3 4   read books or newspapers at a library

_____

b.   1 2 3 4   go shopping (at the mall)

_____

c.   1 2 3 4   play a sport

_____

d.   1 2 3 4   go to a party

_____

e.   1 2 3 4   read books or magazines at a bookstore

_____

f.   1 2 3 4   go to a park

_____

g.   1 2 3 4   go to see a movie

_____

h.   1 2 3 4   be alone in a quiet place for 15 minutes

_____

i.   1 2 3 4   surf the Internet

_____

j.   1 2 3 4   go to a lake or beach

_____

k.   1 2 3 4   talk with friends on the phone

_____

l.   1 2 3 4   be with 3 or 4 friends all day

_____

m.   1 2 3 4   take a walk

_____

n.   1 2 3 4   watch TV

_____

o.   1 2 3 4   visit an art museum

_____

Practice 10B. Group Speaking/Discussion

Now work with a partner. Take turns presenting your answers for the items in Practice 10A. Discuss the points that people have strong opinions for or against.

Pronunciation of -ed in Past Tense

You already know that adding **-ed** forms the past tense of most verbs in English. For example, look at these common verbs:

work—work**ed**   play—play**ed**   want—want**ed**

All of these verbs end in the same two letters: **-ed.** However, the pronunciation of **-ed** in each word is very different. Pronounce these words one more time:

work**ed**   play**ed**   want**ed**

What is the last sound in each of these words?

The word **worked** ends in the sound /t/, the word **played** ends in the sound /d/, and the word **wanted** ends in the sound /id/.

For practice, pronounce these past tense forms and write **t, d,** or **id** to show the sound that you hear.

_____ 1. needed		_____ 4. asked
_____ 2. fixed		_____ 5. called
_____ 3. rained		_____ 6. passed

Check your answers.

• You should have **id** for number one.

• You should have **t** for numbers two, four, and six.

• You should have **d** for numbers three and five.

How many did you get correct? ___

Do you know the rule for past tense pronunciation? Let's do some more examples.

Pronounce these past tense forms and write **t, d,** or **id** to show the past tense pronunciation.

      _____ 1. washed

      _____ 2. worked

      _____ 3. answered

      _____ 4. laughed

      _____ 5. studied

      _____ 6. cleaned

      _____ 7. painted

      _____ 8. added

      _____ 9. watched

      _____ 10. poured

Check your answers.

• You should have **id** for numbers seven and eight.

• You should have **t** for numbers one, two, four, and nine.

• You should have **d** for numbers three, five, six, and ten.

How many did you get correct? ___

Now do you think you know the rule for past tense pronunciation? If you do not know the rule, let's do another practice.

Pronunciation of –ed in Past Tense

Listen to the pronunciation of each verb in this exercise first in present tense and then in past tense. In the first column, write the last sound of the words. In the second column, write **T, D,** or **ID** to show the correct past tense pronunciation.

Past tense practice

Verb	Last sound	Pronunciation	Past tense
1. touch	CH	touch<u>ed</u>	T
2. love	V	lov<u>ed</u>	D
3. like	_____	lik<u>ed</u>	_____
4. mail	_____	mail<u>ed</u>	_____
5. look	_____	look<u>ed</u>	_____
6. decide	_____	decid<u>ed</u>	_____
7. practice	_____	practic<u>ed</u>	_____
8. select	_____	select<u>ed</u>	_____
9. rob	_____	robb<u>ed</u>	_____
10. count	_____	count<u>ed</u>	_____
11. laugh	_____	laugh<u>ed</u>	_____
12. taste	_____	tast<u>ed</u>	_____
13. cough	_____	cough<u>ed</u>	_____
14. stay	_____	stay<u>ed</u>	_____
15. cry	_____	cri<u>ed</u>	_____
16. subtract	_____	subtract<u>ed</u>	_____
17. erase	_____	eras<u>ed</u>	_____
18. close	_____	clos<u>ed</u>	_____
19. dance	_____	danc<u>ed</u>	_____
20. wave	_____	wav<u>ed</u>	_____

General Rule for Past Tense Pronunciation				
	Pronounce:	When the verb ends in these sounds:		
GROUP 1	/t/	/f/	laugh	laughed
		/k/	work	worked
		/p/	help	helped
		/s/	kiss	kissed
		/ch/	touch	touched
		/sh/	wash	washed
GROUP 2	/d/	/b/	rob	robbed
		/g/	hug	hugged
		/j/	judge	judged
		/l/	call	called
		/m/	name	named
		/n/	clean	cleaned
		/r/	pour	poured
		/v/	live	lived
		/z/	close	closed
	All	/ay/	stay	stayed
	Vowels	/ee/	free	freed
		/ie/	lie	lied
		/oy/	enjoy	enjoyed
		/ow/	snow	snowed
GROUP 3	/id/ Extra	/d/	need	needed
	Syllable	/t/	want	wanted

IMPORTANT!   The only time that you will pronounce an extra syllable /id/ is in Group 3. In Group 1 and Group 2, you pronounce an extra sound of either /t/ or /d/.

For practice, how many syllables do these words have?

____ lived   ____ asked   ____ wanted   ____ added

(The answers are, 1, 1, 2, and 2.)

Pronunciation of *-ed* in Past Tense

This exercise has a list of twenty verbs. Pronounce each word, and then decide if the verb has one or two syllables. Write the number 1 or 2 on the line.

Example: YOU HEAR: "needed"

ANSWER: <u>2</u>

Example: YOU HEAR: "passed"

ANSWER: <u>1</u>

1. ___ acted

2. ___ called

3. ___ reached

4. ___ looked

5. ___ tried

6. ___ printed

7. ___ dialed

8. ___ counted

9. ___ crashed

10. ___ ended

11. ___ turned

12. ___ moved

13. ___ started

14. ___ chopped

15. ___ slapped

16. ___ added

17. ___ graded

18. ___ pulled

19. ___ rained

20. ___ peeled

Exercise
13

Present or Past Tense: Sentences about Art as a Hobby

Listen carefully. You will hear a sentence that has one of the two verb forms—present tense or past tense—in parentheses. Underline the word that you hear.

1. Karen and Jim (like, liked) to look at art. This is their main hobby.

2. Yesterday they (walk, walked) to a new art gallery near their house.

3. The workers (open, opened) the art gallery doors at 6 P.M.

4. Sometimes new artists (present, presented) their work for a new gallery opening.

5. Karen and Jim (watch, watched) the presentations.

6. They (listen, listened) to the artists' stories.

7. They (look, looked) at the new paintings and other art.

8. They (talk, talked) to Henry Clemmons, a new artist.

9. He (paints, painted) amazing pictures.

10. At new art gallery openings, people (discuss, discussed) art with the artists.

11. Many people (enjoy, enjoyed) this a great deal.

12. After the presentation, Karen and Jim (help, helped) the artists to pack up their art.

Exercise 14

Tense Recognition: Jigsaw Puzzles as a Hobby

Many people enjoy putting together a jigsaw puzzle as a hobby. Listen carefully. You will hear some sentences about putting together a jigsaw puzzle. Listen for the verb. Choose the verb form that you hear: present tense with *-s*, present tense without *-s*, or past tense with *-ed*—and circle it.

1. help
   helps
   helped

2. want
   wants
   wanted

3. watch
   watches
   watched

4. play
   plays
   played

5. add
   adds
   added

6. start
   starts
   started

7. need
   needs
   needed

8. listen
   listens
   listened

9. prepare
   prepares
   prepared

10. answer
    answers
    answered

<table>
</table>

Exercise
15

Listening Activity: Following Game Results on the Sports Page

Gary is reading the sports page in the newspaper. Listen to the information and then circle the winner of each game. Gary will mention who his favorite baseball team is. After the exercise, try to remember who his favorite team is. (Note: The word **beat** means to win.)

1. Cubs   vs.   Tigers

2. Cleveland   vs.   Seattle

3. Raiders   vs.   Rams

4. Chicago   vs.   Boston

5. Brazil   vs.   Peru

6. Pirates   vs.   Reds

7. Eagles   vs.   Owls

8. Tokyo   vs.   Taipei

9. What is Gary's favorite baseball team? _____

Understanding Simple Lectures: All about Rockets

You will hear a short lecture. This lecture is about Paul's hobby. Listen carefully. After you hear the lecture, read the questions below. Choose the correct answer and put a check (✓) on the line.

1. Which type of hobby rocket does not have a motor?
   —— a. model rocket
   —— b. amateur rocket
   —— c. experimental rocket

2. Which type of rocket does Paul have?
   —— a. model rocket
   —— b. amateur rocket
   —— c. experimental rocket

3. Paul has a government permit for his rocket because
   —— a. his rocket is very large.
   —— b. his rocket can explode.
   —— c. his rocket can go very high.

4. How old was Paul when he started this hobby?
   —— a. 15
   —— b. 45
   —— c. 50

5. What is the highest altitude for Paul's rocket?
   —— a. 503 meters
   —— b. 305 meters
   —— c. 53 meters

Exercise 17

Pair Talking

Work in pairs. Student A works from this page, and student B works from page 116. Take turns describing the pictures with a dot; your partner can listen and ask questions to identify the correct picture and place a dot by the correct picture. Student A describes questions 1, 3, and 5, which are on this page. Student B describes questions 2, 4, and 6, which are on page 116.

A

1.

2.

3.

	30	13	
30	15 50	15	13 50
15 13	50	50	15 30
	13	30	

4.

5.

6.

B

1.

2.

3.

13		30	
15	13 50	15	30 50
50	15 30	50	15 13
30		13	

4.

5.

6.

Exercise
18

Speaking/Discussion: Interviewing Someone about a Hobby

Practice 18A. Preparation

Your task is to interview someone about his or her hobby. Find out the answer to these questions. (You may interview a native English speaker or someone on the Internet. There are many chat rooms where people discuss their hobbies, such as collecting baseball cards or matchbooks.)

1. What is the person's hobby? _____

2. When did this person start this hobby? How? _____

_____

_____

_____

_____

_____

3. How did you meet this person? _____

_____

4. Would you like to take up this hobby? Why or why not? _____

_____

_____

_____

Practice 18B. Group Speaking/Discussion

Now work with a partner or in a group of three to four students. Take turns discussing your responses to the questions in Practice 18A.

Rapid Vocabulary Review

From the three answers on the right, circle the one that **best explains, is an example of,** or **combines with** the vocabulary word on the left.

VOCABULARY		ANSWERS	
1. **grade**	a. B+	b. 3/82	c. 37°
2. **pull**	a. with your hand	b. with a computer	c. with a few dollars
3. **quiet**	a. no color	b. no noise	c. no books
4. **rob**	a. need money	b. take money	c. give money
5. **seasons**	a. team	b. rocket	c. fall
6. **take up**	a. a pet	b. a walk	c. a hobby
7. **taste**	a. trade	b. sweet	c. high
8. **touch**	a. toast	b. stay	c. finger
9. **uncle**	a. team	b. male	c. fuel
10. **work out**	a. belong	b. crash	c. gym
11. **the ground**	a. carrots	b. issues	c. popcorn
12. **lake**	a. water	b. mountain	c. land
13. **liquid**	a. cream	b. sugar	c. rice
14. **magazine**	a. store	b. read	c. laugh
15. **meal**	a. lose	b. eat	c. mail
16. **over twenty**	a. 19	b. 20	c. 21
17. **peel**	a. a banana	b. a poster	c. a party
18. **act**	a. achieve	b. behave	c. believe
19. **album**	a. altitudes	b. pictures	c. cans
20. **alone**	a. 0 people	b. 1 person	c. 2 people
21. **amount**	a. feeling	b. person	c. number
22. **capital**	a. time	b. place	c. person
23. **coin**	a. color	b. feeling	c. money
24. **cough**	a. a car	b. a person	c. a day
25. **dial**	a. telephone	b. photograph	c. refrigerator

MORE VOCABULARY PRACTICE ON THE WEB

Go to the activities for unit 4 at www.press.umich.edu/esl/compsite/
targetinglistening/ and do the five vocabulary exercises there. Record
your scores here. The best score in each exercise is 20.

Quiz 4.1. Your Score _____ / 20 _____

Quiz 4.2. Your Score _____ / 20 _____

Quiz 4.3. Your Score _____ / 20 _____

Quiz 4.4. Your Score _____ / 20 _____

Quiz 4.5. Your Score _____ / 20 _____

Spending Money

Exercise 1

Listening Activity: Understanding Messages about Spending Money

You will hear information about three people. They are each talking about buying something. Listen carefully. On the line, write what each person is talking about buying.

Part 1   What is each person talking about buying?

1. _____

2. _____

3. _____

Part 2   Now listen to the questions for number 4, 5, and 6. Write your answers on the lines.

4. _____

5. _____

6. _____

Exercise 2

Dictation in a Dialogue: Trying to Get a Better Price (bargaining)

This is a dialogue in which the people are **bargaining**. **Bargaining** means when you try to get a better price for something that you want to buy. The people in the dialogue are friends talking about the price of a car.

There are seven blank lines in the dialogue. Fill in each blank line with the correct sentence that you will hear.

Listen carefully. You will hear a number. Find that sentence number. You will hear each sentence three times. First, listen to the sentence. Repeat the sentence. Then listen again. Write the sentence. Finally, listen again. Check your sentence. The number in the parentheses is the number of words in the sentence. Do not spell out numbers. Use numbers, not words. A number counts as one word. For example, $9,000 counts as one word. Now, let's begin with number 1.

Liz: Do you like my car?

Megan: Yes, I do. How much is it again?

Liz: ❶ _____ (4)

Megan: That is a lot of money. Do you think you can make a lower price?

Liz: Well, I'm not sure. ❷ _____ (8)

Megan: I was thinking of paying $9,000 plus giving you the painting in my living room. What do you think of that idea?

Liz: Which painting is it?

Megan: ❸ _____
           _____ (11)

Liz: Oh, I love that painting. Hmm . . . , what if you paid me $9,500 and the painting?

Megan: ❹ _____ (9)

Liz: Chocolate chip?

Megan: Your favorite.

Liz: OK, it's a deal! **5** _____

_____ (6)

Megan: **6** _____

_____ (12)

Liz: **7** _____ (9)

Megan: Great! I will call my husband right now and tell him the good news!

Extra Practice. **Listening Practice**

Close your books. Listen to the complete dialogue from Exercise 2. If there is any part that you cannot understand well, listen to that part again. (Try to listen to this dialogue without looking at your book. This is a good way to improve your listening.)

Extra Practice. **Dialogue Practice**

Work in pairs. Look at Exercise 2 again. Each person will be one of the characters in the dialogue. Read the dialogue as the characters. When you have finished, change characters and read it one more time. After you have finished, you may want to listen to the recording of the dialogue one more time.

Exercise 3

Recognition of *was* and *were* in Questions about a Purchase

Congratulations! You wanted to buy a motorcycle for a long time, and you finally bought one! In this exercise, people will ask you questions about you and your new purchase. These questions begin with **Was** or with **Were.** Circle the word that begins the question.

1.	Was	Were		6.	Was	Were
2.	Was	Were		7.	Was	Were
3.	Was	Were		8.	Was	Were
4.	Was	Were		9.	Was	Were
5.	Was	Were		10.	Was	Were

Mathematics	(Math)	
Addition	12 + 8 = 20	12 + 8 —— 20

ADD 12 and 8
12 and 8 are 20
12 plus 8 is 20

Subtraction	18 − 5 = 13	18 − 5 —— 13

SUBTRACT 5 from 18.
18 minus 5 is 13.
18 take away 5 is 13.

Multiplication	10 × 3 = 30	10 × 3 —— 30

MULTIPLY 10 by 3.
10 times 3 is 30.

Division	20 ÷ 4 = 5	$4\overline{)20}^{\,5}$

DIVIDE 20 by 4.
20 divided by 4 is 5.
4 goes into 20 5 times.

Exercise 4

Understanding Simple Math Problems

You will hear a math problem. Write in the missing numbers in the correct places.

1. ◯
    + ◯
    ———
      26

2. ◯
    + 6
    ———
    ◯

3.   13
    + ◯
    ———
    ◯

4. ◯
    + 7
    ———
    ◯

5. ◯
    − 5
    ———
    ◯

6. ◯
    − 17
    ———
    ◯

7.   25
    − ◯
    ———
    ◯

8. ◯
    − 2
    ———
    ◯

9. ◯
    × 3
    ———
    ◯

10. ◯
    × 2
    ———
    ◯

11. ◯ ÷ 4 = ◯   or   4⟌◯ (quotient ◯)

12. ◯ ÷ ◯ = 9   or   ◯⟌◯ (quotient 9)

Understanding Numbers in Number Situations

In this exercise, you will hear situations involving numbers. Listen very carefully to each situation. Take notes on the information and then answer the question about the situation. Each situation and question will be repeated.

Example: YOU HEAR: "I have eight books. I gave one book to Jerry and two books to Jerry's brother. Question: How many books do I have now?"

ANSWER: ___5___

1. _____   7. _____

2. _____   8. _____

3. _____   9. _____

4. _____   10. _____

5. _____   11. _____

6. _____   12. _____

Exercise 6

Speaking/Discussion: The Most Expensive* Thing That You've Bought

Practice 6A. Preparation

Read these questions about money. Write your answers to the questions on the lines provided.

1. What is the most expensive thing that you ever bought? _____

2. Where did you buy this item? _____

3. When did you buy it? _____

4. Why was this item important to you? In other words, why did you buy something that was so expensive?

_____

_____

_____

_____

_____

_____

5. In hindsight, was it a good thing to buy this item? In other words, if you could go back in time, would you buy that item again?

_____

_____

_____

_____

_____

_____

*Instead of the most expensive item, you could talk about the most unusual purchase.

Practice 6B. Group Speaking/Discussion

Now work with a partner or in a group of three to four students. Take turns discussing your responses to the questions in Practice 6A. Listen carefully. Do you think each person's purchase was a good one? Was it necessary? Would you buy that item? Why or why not?

Exercise

7

Affirmative vs. Negative: *was, were* about a Trip

Tim recently spent several hundred dollars for a trip. He took a vacation in Dallas, Texas. He flew from Los Angeles to Dallas. He stayed in a nice hotel. He ate at nice restaurants. Listen carefully. You will hear some statements about Tim's trip. All of the statements use ***was, wasn't, were,*** or ***weren't***. If the statement is affirmative (***was*** or ***were***), circle the plus sign (+). If the statement is negative (***wasn't*** or ***weren't***), circle the negative sign (−).

Example: YOU HEAR: "The trip was great."

ANSWER: (+)   −

1.	+	−	6.	+	−
2.	+	−	7.	+	−
3.	+	−	8.	+	−
4.	+	−	9.	+	−
5.	+	−	10.	+	−

Understanding Simple Conversations: Buying a Vehicle

You will hear a short conversation between Carla and a car salesperson named Ricardo. In this conversation, the salesperson Ricardo will describe a new vehicle to Carla. Listen carefully. After you hear the conversation, read the questions below. Choose the correct answer and put a check (✓) on the line.

1. What did Carla think about the truck?
   ____ a. It was small.
   ____ b. It was big.
   ____ c. It was cheap.

2. Where did Carla and Ricardo go on their test drive?
   ____ a. to the city
   ____ b. to Barnes Street
   ____ c. to Barton Blvd.

3. Who has a horse trailer?
   ____ a. Ricardo
   ____ b. Ricardo's brother
   ____ c. Carla

4. Where does Ricardo want to talk about the price of the car?
   ____ a. at Smith's Auto Center
   ____ b. in the truck during the test drive
   ____ c. in his office

5. Why did Carla say she wants a good price?
   ____ a. because she is a student
   ____ b. because she is a car salesperson
   ____ c. because she is not working now

Exercise
9

Using Short Answers for Yes-No Questions about Cell Phones

Listen carefully to these sentences about cell phones. You will hear a question. Choose the correct answer, and circle the letter of that answer.

1. a. No, they weren't.
   b. No, it wasn't.
   c. No, he wasn't.

2. a. No, they weren't.
   b. No, she wasn't.
   c. No, he wasn't.

3. a. Yes, they were.
   b. Yes, I was.
   c. Yes, we were.

4. a. No, I wasn't.
   b. No, he wasn't.
   c. No, we weren't.

5. a. Yes, he was.
   b. Yes, she was.
   c. Yes, they were.

6. a. Yes, you were.
   b. Yes, I was.
   c. Yes, we were.

7. a. No, they weren't.
   b. No, she wasn't.
   c. No, it wasn't.

8. a. Yes, they were.
   b. Yes, there was.
   c. Yes, you were.

9. a. Yes, they were.
   b. Yes, he was.
   c. Yes, it was.

10. a. No, it wasn't.
    b. No, we weren't.
    c. No, she wasn't.

Exercise 10

Answering *Where/When* Questions about Things We Buy

You will hear some questions about things that people buy. All of the questions begin with ***where*** or ***when***. Listen carefully to the question and then put a check mark (✓) by the best answer.

1. ___ a. at one o'clock
   ___ b. on the computer

2. ___ a. on the table
   ___ b. an hour ago

3. ___ a. near the tree
   ___ b. last night

4. ___ a. in the yard
   ___ b. on Monday

5. ___ a. at the bank
   ___ b. at seven A.M.

6. ___ a. in the bedroom
   ___ b. right now

7. ___ a. in five minutes
   ___ b. by the window

8. ___ a. in the afternoon
   ___ b. here

9. ___ a. last Friday
   ___ b. at the library

10. ___ a. next week
    ___ b. in the store

11. ___ a. on Thursday
    ___ b. on Green Street

12. ___ a. at noon on Monday
    ___ b. in a store in Maine

Spelling Common Letter Combinations

Listen carefully. You will hear three letters. The three letters do not spell a word. They are only three letters. Write the letters that you hear. This is a rapid exercise.

1. _____	6. _____	11. _____
2. _____	7. _____	12. _____
3. _____	8. _____	13. _____
4. _____	9. _____	14. _____
5. _____	10. _____	15. _____

Exercise
12

Speaking/Discussion: Saving up Money for Something Special

Practice 12A. Preparation

Imagine that you want to buy a used car. You have some money, but it's not enough. You still need an additional $4,000. You have six months or so to come up with this money. What are some ways to save money during that time? Think of at least five ways to save money during this time. (For example, you might write "Eat at home more often.")

1. _____

_____

2. _____

_____

3. _____

_____

4. _____

_____

5. _____

_____

Practice 12B. Group Speaking/Discussion

Now work with a partner. Take turns presenting your suggestions for ways to save money. Are there any similarities in your suggestions and your partner's suggestions? When you have finished, change partners and start again for more practice and more ideas.

Rows and Columns		
Square	A square has four equal sides.	
Row	A horizontal line	←HORIZONTAL→
Column	A vertical line	↑ V E R T I C A L ↓

Left Column	Middle Column	Right Column
1	**2**	**3**
4	**5**	**6**
7	**8**	**9**

Boxes 1, 2, and 3 are in the <u>top row</u>.
Boxes 4, 5, and 6 are in the <u>middle row</u>.
Boxes 7, 8, and 9 are in the <u>bottom row</u>.

Square 1 top row, left column
Square 2 top row, middle column
Square 3 top row, right column
Square 4 middle row, left column
Square 5 middle row, middle column
Square 6 middle row, right column

Square 7 bottom row, left column
Square 8 bottom row, middle column
Square 9 bottom row, right column

Another word for **square** is **box.**
Another word for **middle** is **center.**

Exercise 13

Following Directions (rows and columns)

Listen carefully to the instructions. Find the correct square. Write the correct information in the square. The first square is already completed for you.

	N	

Exercise 14

Following Directions (rows and columns)

Listen carefully to the instructions. Find the correct square. Write the correct information in the square. The first square is already completed for you.

✔		

Listening Activity: What Is Your Advice?

Listen carefully. In this exercise, you are a talk show host on a radio show. Your job is to listen to people's problems and offer some advice to help. In this exercise, a person will call the radio station and ask you, the expert, for your advice. After you hear the problem and understand it, write your advice on the line. You may want to listen to the problem more than once.

Dear Confused, _____

_____

_____

_____ .

_____

_____

_____

_____

_____

_____ .

Now, with a partner, discuss your answer. After discussing, whose advice do you think is better?

Exercise
16

Recognition of Sounds /b/ and /v/ in Words

You will hear one word. The word has the sound of either **B** or **V** at the beginning, middle, or end of the word. Write the letter of the sound that you hear.

Beginning	**Middle**	**End**
1. ——	8. ——	15. ——
2. ——	9. ——	16. ——
3. ——	10. ——	17. ——
4. ——	11. ——	18. ——
5. ——	12. ——	19. ——
6. ——	13. ——	20. ——
7. ——	14. ——	

For extra practice, can you think of more examples?

Beginning	**Middle**	**End**
1. ——	4. ——	7. ——
2. ——	5. ——	8. ——
3. ——	6. ——	9. ——

Exercise 17

Recognition of Sounds /b/ and /v/ in Words in Sentences

Look at the list of words below. You will hear a sentence that has one of these words. Circle the word that you hear.

1. bet   vet   6. boat   vote

2. boat   vote   7. berry   very

3. bet   vet   8. bend   vend

4. best   vest   9. beer   veer

5. boys   voice   10. berry   very

Exercise 18

Pair Talking

Work in pairs. Student A works from this page, and student B works from page 142. Take turns describing the pictures with a dot; your partner can listen and ask questions to identify the correct picture and place a dot by the correct picture. Student A describes questions 1, 3, and 5, which are on this page. Student B describes questions 2, 4, and 6, which are on page 142.

A

1.

2. | 12 − 4 = | 12 + 4 = | 12 ÷ 4 = | 12 x 4 = |

3.

4.

5. | 30 <br> x 13
 ———
 390 | 13 <br> x 30
 ———
 390 | 13 x 30 = 390 | 30 x 13 = 390 |

6.

B

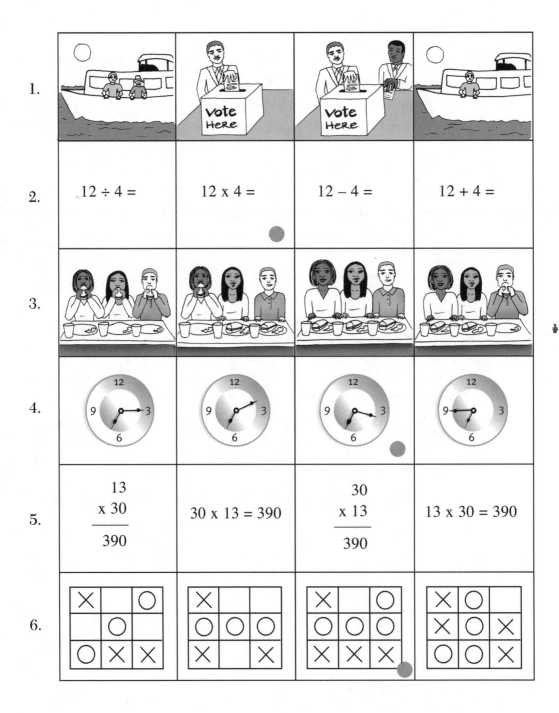

1.

2.

| 12 ÷ 4 = | 12 x 4 = | 12 − 4 = | 12 + 4 = |

3.

4.

5.

| 13
x 30
———
390 | 30 x 13 = 390 | 30
x 13
———
390 | 13 x 30 = 390 |

6.

Exercise

19

Understanding Simple Lectures: Saving Up Money for the Future

You will hear a short lecture. Most of the discussions in this unit are about spending money, but the topic of this lecture is saving money. Listen carefully. After you hear the lecture, read the questions below. Choose the correct answer and put a check (✓) on the line.

1. What percentage did the speaker mention in the example?
    ____ a. 6%
    ____ b. 16%
    ____ c. 60%

2. In the example of compounding, when will you have $1,340?
    ____ a. three years
    ____ b. five years
    ____ c. ten years

3. What is $2,500 in this example?
    ____ a. your savings without compounding
    ____ b. your savings at the end of ten years
    ____ c. your savings minus the $1,000

4. What does the speaker say is the most important thing in saving for the future?
    ____ a. put a lot of money in the bank
    ____ b. start saving money early
    ____ c. wait at least 25 years before you spend the money

5. At the end of 25 years, with 6% growth with compounding, how much will $1,000 be?
    ____ a. $1,400
    ____ b. $3,400
    ____ c. $4,300

Exercise 20

Speaking/Discussion: Advice on Buying the Best Gift

Practice 20A. Preparation

What is the best gift for a person? Read the description of these four people. With a budget of $50 per person, what gift would you recommend for each person? (It is OK to suggest more than one possibility.) What thing do you have to consider in each case? Write two or three sentences to explain your gift selection.

SITUATION 1	**SITUATION 2**
PERSON: your grandmother	PERSON: your neighbor's daughter
COMMENTS: She is 88 years old. You love your grandmother very much. She lives alone and has almost everything she needs.	COMMENTS: She is 17 years old and is graduating from high school next week. This gift will be a high school graduation gift.
GIFT: _____	GIFT: _____
REASON: _____	REASON: _____
_____	_____
_____	_____
_____	_____
SITUATION 3	**SITUATION 4**
PERSON: your boss	PERSON: your best friend
COMMENTS: You get along well with her. It's her birthday. She likes to read, but you aren't sure what subjects she likes.	COMMENTS: He/She likes tourism and travel, but with $50, you cannot buy an airplane ticket for any destination.
GIFT: _____	GIFT: _____
REASON: _____	REASON: _____
_____	_____
_____	_____
_____	_____

Practice 20B. Group Speaking/Discussion

Now work with a partner or in a group of three to four students. Take turns discussing your responses to the questions in Practice 20A.

Exercise 21. Rapid Vocabulary Review

From the three answers on the right, circle the one that **best explains, is an example of,** or **combines with** the vocabulary word on the left.

VOCABULARY	ANSWERS		
1. **boss**	a. at work	b. at school	c. at home
2. **expensive**	a. much money	b. much time	c. much pressure
3. **get along**	a. with time	b. with people	c. with vocabulary
4. **almost 100**	a. 90–99; 101–110	b. 80–89; 111–120	c. 70–79; 121–130
5. **budget**	a. birthday	b. money	c. food
6. **pillow**	a. on a bed	b. on a floor	c. on a table
7. **a case**	a. situation	b. comment	c. destination
8. **catch**	a. a gift	b. a ball	c. a card
9. **graduate**	a. from work	b. from school	c. from party
10. **living room**	a. in a house	b. in a hotel	c. in a travel office
11. **low**	a. not final	b. not special	c. not high
12. **65 is lower __**	a. than 90	b. than 60	c. than 30
13. **neighbor**	a. place	b. item	c. person
14. **subject**	a. math	b. ticket	c. purchase
15. **I suggest**	a. my need	b. my idea	c. my bargain
16. **10 goes into 80**	a. 800 times	b. 90 times	c. 8 times
17. **How much is __ ?**	a. cost	b. suggest	c. almost
18. **in hindsight**	a. yesterday	b. tomorrow	c. next year
19. **congratulations**	a. good news	b. usual item	c. instead of yes
20. **daughter**	a. male	b. female	c. male and female
21. **division**	a. $2 \times 4 = 8$	b. $8 \div 2 = 4$	c. $8 - 2 = 6$
22. **equal sign**	a. $+$	b. $=$	c. $-$
23. **best**	a. very good	b. good	c. a little good
24. **everything**	a. 100%	b. 80%	c. 60%
25. **advice**	a. your ideas	b. your purchases	c. your items

MORE VOCABULARY PRACTICE ON THE WEB

Go to the activities for unit 5 at www.press.umich.edu/esl/compsite/targetinglistening/ and do the five vocabulary exercises there. Record your scores here. The best score in each exercise is 20.

Quiz 5.1. Your Score _____ / 20 _____

Quiz 5.2. Your Score _____ / 20 _____

Quiz 5.3. Your Score _____ / 20 _____

Quiz 5.4. Your Score _____ / 20 _____

Quiz 5.5. Your Score _____ / 20 _____

Family and Friends

Exercise

1

Listening Activity: Filling in a Family Tree

This is Anna's family tree. Listen carefully to the information. Write the names of Anna's family members in the correct spaces in the family tree. Look at the box with six names in it. These are the names of six of Anna's family members. Repeat each name: Ben, Carina, Carlos, Eva, Julia, Patricia.

Now listen to the six clues that will help you fill in the names in the correct places on the family tree.

Family Names: Ben, Carina, Carlos, Eva, Julia, Patricia, José, Peter, Max

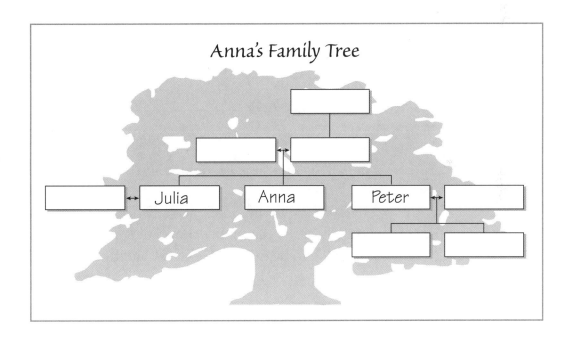

Exercise
2

Dictation in a Dialogue: "Long Time No See"

This dialogue is a conversation between two family members. The people have not been in touch with each other in a long time.

There are seven blanks in the dialogue. Fill in each blank line with the correct sentence that you will hear.

Listen carefully. You will hear a number. Find that sentence number. You will hear each sentence three times. First, listen to the sentence. Repeat the sentence. Then listen again. Write the sentence. Finally, listen again. Check your sentence. The number in parentheses is the number of words in the sentence.

Jackie: Hi, Ellen. This is your cousin Jackie calling from New York.

Ellen: Jackie! Hi, how are you? ❶ _____

_____ . (7) How have you been?

Jackie: I'm doing great. ❷ _____

_____ . (5) How's your mom?

Ellen: She's fine. She's at work right now. ❸ _____

_____ . (6)

Jackie: OK. Ellen, the reason that I'm calling now is to tell you that I'm going to be in New York next month, and if you're free, I'd like to have lunch with you.

Ellen: Sure. ❹ _____ . (3)
When will you be here?

Jackie: At the beginning of October. ❺ _____

_____ . (8) I'm going there on business, and my company hasn't told me the exact dates yet.

Ellen: Well, when you know the dates that you'll be here, call me back

and let's make a specific plan. ❻ _____

_____ ! (7)

Jackie: I agree! And I really want to see your mom. **7** _____

_____. (11)

Ellen: What a great surprise! Please let us know when you'll be here so we can take you somewhere special for lunch.

Extra Practice. **Listening Practice**

Close your books. Listen to the complete dialogue from Exercise 2. If there is any part that you cannot understand well, listen to that part again. (Try to listen to this dialogue without looking at your book. This is a good way to improve your listening.)

Extra Practice. **Dialogue Practice**

Work in pairs. Look at Exercise 2 again. Each person will be one of the characters in the dialogue. Read the dialogue as the characters. When you have finished, change characters and read it again. After you have finished, you may want to listen to the recording of the dialogue one more time.

Exercise 3

Recognition of *am/is/are/was/were/do/does/did* **in Yes-No Questions about a Family**

Sammi is showing her family tree to Mark. Mark is asking Sammi some questions about Sammi's family. Listen carefully to Mark's questions. Write the word that begins Mark's questions.

1. _____   6. _____   11. _____

2. _____   7. _____   12. _____

3. _____   8. _____   13. _____

4. _____   9. _____   14. _____

5. _____   10. _____   15. _____

Numbers: -teen/-ty

Sometimes it is difficult to understand numbers in English. You may have problems with the difference between 13 and 30, 14 and 40, or 15 and 50.

The numbers 13, 14, 15, 16, 17, 18, and 19 are easy to pronounce. These numbers have two equal syllables. For example, thirteen has emphasis on both syllables: thir/teen.

The numbers 20, 30, 40, 50, 60, 70, 80, and 90 are a little more difficult to pronounce. These numbers have two syllables, but the syllables do not have equal stress. In these numbers, there is strong emphasis on the first syllable: thir/ty.

13	thir/teen	30	thir/ty
14	four/teen	40	for/ty
15	fif/teen	50	fif/ty
16	six/teen	60	six/ty
17	seven/teen	70	seven/ty
18	eigh/teen	80	eigh/ty
19	nine/teen	90	nine/ty

13 14 15 16 17 18 19: These numbers have two equal parts. You pronounce each part the same.

30 40 50 60 70 80 90: These numbers have two parts also, but the two parts are not equal. You pronounce the first part very loud, and the second part is very, very short.

There is one other difference between these two groups of numbers (in American English). In one group, you can hear the sound /t/ in the middle very strongly. In the other group, the /t/ sound is very small.

Strong /t/: 13 14 15 16 17 18 19

Weak /t/: 30 40 50 60 70 80 90

Recognition of Numbers (*-teen/-ty*) within a Sentence

In this exercise, you will hear a sentence. Underline the number that you hear.

1. My uncle dropped (16, 60) cents.

2. Dad's birthday is in (13, 30) days.

3. Mom studied for (14, 40) hours.

4. There were (19, 90) guests at Adriane's wedding.

5. Dan has (15, 50) pencils in his desk.

6. My cousin was married for (15, 50) years.

7. The temperature at my cousin Mike's graduation was (18, 80) degrees.

8. Grandma has about (15, 50) plants in her garden.

9. I need (16, 60) dollars to buy that book.

10. In my sister's reading class, there are (13, 30) students.

11. Aunt Candida's dog weighs (17, 70) pounds.

12. My cousin Charlie has (15, 50) marbles.

13. My nephew Nicholas didn't sleep for (19, 90) hours.

14. Dad has (18, 80) model airplanes in his collection.

15. My mother's cell phone provides (114, 140) free minutes per week.

Exercise
5

Recognition of Numbers (-*teen*/-*ty*) within a Sentence

In this exercise, you will hear a sentence. Listen carefully for the number that you hear. Write the number in numeral form on the line.

1. _____   6. _____   11. _____   16. _____

2. _____   7. _____   12. _____   17. _____

3. _____   8. _____   13. _____   18. _____

4. _____   9. _____   14. _____   19. _____

5. _____   10. _____   15. _____   20. _____

Exercise 6

Speaking/Discussion: Talking about Your Family Tree

Practice 6A. Preparation

Draw your family tree in this space. Include your parents, grandparents, brothers, sisters, aunts, uncles, cousins, nephews, nieces, grandchildren, and in-laws.

Practice 6B. Group Speaking/Discussion

Now work with a partner or in a group of three to four students. Take turns talking about your family trees. After each person presents his or her tree, the other students should ask questions such as, "Do you have any other cousins?" or "What does your uncle do for a living?" or "How many of your family members live in the same city?" or "When is the last time you saw your nephew?"

Exercise 7

Answering Yes-No Questions about Family Members

Listen carefully. You will hear a question related to a family member. Choose the correct answer, and circle the letter of that answer.

1. a. Yes, it was.
   b. Yes, it is.
   c. Yes, it does.

2. a. Yes, they did.
   b. Yes, they are.
   c. Yes, they do.

3. a. No, we weren't.
   b. No, we aren't.
   c. No, we don't.

4. a. Yes, I am.
   b. Yes, I was.
   c. Yes, I did.

5. a. No, she doesn't.
   b. No, she wasn't.
   c. No, she was.

6. a. Yes, it did.
   b. Yes, it was.
   c. Yes, it does.

7. a. Yes, he was.
   b. Yes, he does.
   c. Yes, he did.

8. a. Yes, I do.
   b. Yes, I am.
   c. Yes, I did.

9. a. No, he didn't.
   b. No, he don't.
   c. No, he wasn't.

10. a. Yes, she does.
    b. Yes, she was.
    c. Yes, she did.

Exercise 8

Answering *Who* or *What* Questions about Family Members

Listen carefully to the questions about family members. Each question begins with **Who** or **What.** Circle the letter of the best answer for each question that you hear.

1. a. a new watch
   b. my little nephew

2. a. a chair
   b. a cousin

3. a. my family
   b. Thanksgiving

4. a. going to the beach
   b. my uncle Louie

5. a. Shirley
   b. rice with beans

6. a. mushrooms and pepperoni
   b. my nephew and my niece

7. a. rice pudding
   b. a waiter

8. a. Hoffman
   b. a good grade

9. a. I like my new boss.
   b. Suzanne Moore.

10. a. my reading book
    b. my best friend

Exercise 9

Speaking/Discussion: Talking about Your Family Members

Practice 9A. Preparation

Answer these three questions about your family members. Later you will discuss this information with your classmates. Remember that family here means your extended family, which includes cousins, aunts, uncles, nephews, nieces, in-laws, and grandparents.

1. The oldest person in your family

   a. What is the person's name? _____

   b. What is the person's relationship to you? _____

   c. How old is this person? _____

   d. In what year was this person born? _____

   e. Can you think of some things that happened in your country or

      the world in that same year? _____

      _____

2. The most interesting person in your family

   a. What is the person's name? _____

   b. What is the person's relationship to you? _____

   c. What makes this person so interesting? _____

      _____

      _____

      _____

3. The most influential family member on your life

   a. What is the person's name? _____

   b. What is the person's relationship to you? _____

   c. How has this person influenced your life? _____

     _____

     _____

     _____

     _____

4. Your brothers and sisters

   a. How many brothers and sisters do you have? _____

   b. How many brothers and sisters should a child have? Or do you think that being an only child is an advantage? For this question, give reasons from your own life.

     _____

     _____

     _____

     _____

     _____

     _____

Practice 9B. Group Speaking/Discussion

Now work with a partner or in a small group of three to four students. Take turns talking about your answers about your family. Discuss the information one question at a time. After everyone has contributed information and feedback about question number one, then move to number two, and so on.

Understanding Simple Conversations: Introducing a Friend

You will hear a short conversation between Jim and his mother. In this conversation, Jim will introduce his friend Kyle to his mother. Listen carefully. After you hear the conversation, read the questions below. Choose the correct answer and put a check (✓) on the line.

1. Where is Kyle from?
   ___ a. New York
   ___ b. Miami
   ___ c. London

2. Kyle is on vacation with his
   ___ a. sister.
   ___ b. friend Jim.
   ___ c. parents.

3. Where is Jim's mother going?
   ___ a. to her friend's house
   ___ b. to the bank
   ___ c. to a game

4. Where is Jim going?
   ___ a. on vacation
   ___ b. to the bank
   ___ c. to a game

5. When does the game start?
   ___ a. at 10 o'clock
   ___ b. in 10 minutes
   ___ c. 10 minutes ago

Days and Months

Days of the week
Sunday
Monday
Tuesday
Wednesday
Thursday
Friday
Saturday

Months of the year
January
February
March
April
May
June
July
August
September
October
November
December

Exercise 11

Recognition of the Days of the Week within Sentences

Listen carefully. You will hear a sentence that has the name of a day of the week. Write the day that you hear on the line.

Example: YOU HEAR: "My cousins will drive to New York on Tuesday."

ANSWER: <u>Tuesday</u>

1. _____   6. _____

2. _____   7. _____

3. _____   8. _____

4. _____   9. _____

5. _____   10. _____

Exercise 12

Recognition of the Months of the Year within Sentences

Listen carefully. You will hear a sentence that has the name of a month of the year. Write the month that you hear on the line.

Example: YOU HEAR: "July is a very hot month."

ANSWER: <u>July</u>

1. _____   6. _____

2. _____   7. _____

3. _____   8. _____

4. _____   9. _____

5. _____   10. _____

Exercise 13

Following Directions (rows and columns)

Listen carefully to the instructions. You will hear the information two times. Find the correct square. Write the correct information in the square. The first square is already completed for you.

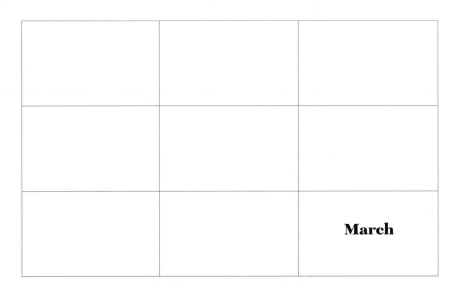

		March

Exercise 14

Following Directions (rows and columns)

Listen carefully to the instructions. You will hear the information two times. Find the correct square. Write the correct information in the square. The first square is already completed for you.

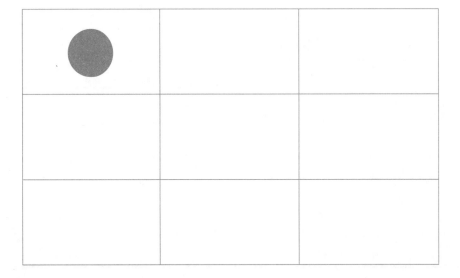

Exercise 15

Sound Practice: /ch/ and /sh/

This is a rapid exercise. You will hear one word. Write the letters **CH** or the letters **SH** on the line to indicate the sound that you hear in that word.

Example: YOU HEAR: "wish"

ANSWER: ___SH___

Beginning

1. _____
2. _____
3. _____
4. _____
5. _____
6. _____
7. _____
8. _____
9. _____

Middle

10. _____
11. _____
12. _____
13. _____
14. _____

End

15. _____
16. _____
17. _____
18. _____
19. _____
20. _____

For extra practice, can you think of more examples?

Beginning

1. _____
2. _____
3. _____

Middle

4. _____
5. _____
6. _____

End

7. _____
8. _____
9. _____

Exercise
16

Sound Practice: /ch/ and /sh/ (minimal pairs in sentences)

Look at the list of words below. You will hear a sentence that has one of these words. Circle the word that you hear.

Example: YOU HEAR: "He wants to catch some fish."

             ANSWER: (catch)   cash

1. teacher   T-shirt

2. witch   wish

3. chair   share

4. cheap   sheep

5. chin   shin

6. watcher   washer

7. match   mash

8. chew   shoe

9. cheese   she's

10. chip   ship

Exercise

17

Short Conversations (details)

You will hear three short conversations. After each conversation, you will hear three or four questions. Answer the questions based on the information in the conversations.

Conversation 1

1. a. Ann   c. Sue
   b. Anna   d. Susan

2. a. sisters   c. friends
   b. parents   d. strangers

3. a. She had a birthday.
   b. She ate a special dinner.
   c. She bought a new CD player.

Conversation 2

4. a. Kevin's brother   c. Paul's brother
   b. Kevin's cousin   d. Paul's cousin

5. a. talking on the phone   c. looking at a photo
   b. chatting on the Internet   d. talking about his own brother

6. a. two   c. four
   b. three   d. five

Conversation 3

7. a. cousins   c. niece/aunt
   b. sisters   d. mother/daughter

8. a. Laura   b. Vanessa

9. a. take a trip   c. have a family party
   b. have lunch   d. do some business

10. a. September   c. November
    b. October   d. December

Understanding Simple Lectures: A Family Reunion

You will hear a short lecture. This lecture is about family reunions. Listen carefully. After you hear the lecture, read the questions below. Choose the correct answer and put a check (✓) on the line.

1. How often does a family reunion occur?
   —— a. every few months
   —— b. every few years
   —— c. every other year

2. Where are family reunions usually held?
   —— a. at a family member's house or a hotel
   —— b. at an expensive restaurant
   —— c. on a large boat

3. Who is the leader of a family reunion?
   —— a. a professional person
   —— b. a younger family member
   —— c. a senior family member

4. What is the main purpose of a family reunion?
   —— a. make business connections
   —— b. vacation activities
   —— c. keep family connections close

5. When a family reunion ends, people are sad, but what do they look forward to?
   —— a. the next family reunion
   —— b. returning home
   —— c. a vacation

Exercise 19

Pair Talking

Work in pairs. Student A works from this page, and student B works from page 170. Take turns describing the pictures with a dot; your partner can listen and ask questions to identify the correct picture and place a dot by the correct picture. Student A describes questions 1, 3, and 5, which are on this page. Student B describes questions 2, 4, and 6, which are on page 170.

A

1.				
2.	30 15 / 50 13	13 50 / 15 30	30 50 / 15 13	13 15 / 50 30
3.				
4.	I'm 13 I'm 15	I'm 13 I'm 15	I'm 13 I'm 15	I'm 13 I'm 15
5.	thirteen 13 15 fifteen	15 fifteen 13 thirteen	fifteen 15 thirteen 13	thirteen 13 fifteen 15
6.	Sun. Mon. Tues.	SUNDAY MONDAY TUESDAY	Sunday Monday Tuesday	Sunday Monday Tuesday

B

1.				
2.	13 50 / 15 30	30 15 / 50 13	13 15 / 50 30	30 50 / 15 13
3.				
4.	I'm 13 I'm 15	I'm 13 I'm 15	I'm 13 I'm 15	I'm 13 I'm 15
5.	thirteen 13 fifteen 15	thirteen 13 15 fifteen	15 fifteen 13 thirteen	fifteen 15 thirteen 13
6.	Sunday Monday Tuesday	Sunday Monday Tuesday	SUNDAY MONDAY TUESDAY	Sun. Mon. Tues.

Exercise
20

Speaking/Discussion: Common Last Names in the United States

Practice 20A. Preparation

Look at this list of the ten most common
family names in the United States.*

Brown	Moore
Davis	Smith
Johnson	Taylor
Jones	Williams
Miller	Wilson

Based on your knowledge of last names in English, arrange these names
in order from the most common to the tenth most common.

1. _____   6. _____

2. _____   7. _____

3. _____   8. _____

4. _____   9. _____

5. _____   10. _____

Practice 20B. Group Speaking/Discussion

Now work with a partner or in a group of three to four students. Take
turns presenting your list from Practice 20A and then compare your
answers. Try to get everyone in your group to agree on a final group list.
When finished, check your answers with your teacher.

(**Note:** For additional practice, add details when you talk about these
names. Who do you know that has one of these last names? For
example: My neighbor's last name is Miller. Describe the person with
as much detail as you can with your partner.)

*From: www.census.gov/genealogy/www/freqnames.html

Exercise 21

Rapid Vocabulary Review

From the three answers on the right, circle the one that **best explains, is an example of,** or **combines with** the vocabulary word on the left.

VOCABULARY	ANSWERS		
1. **establish**	a. a new school	b. a small problem	c. an important issue
2. **every other number**	a. 1 3 5 7 9	b. 2 6 10 14 18	c. 5 4 3 2 1
3. **farm**	a. students	b. animals	c. rooms
4. **square**	a. 3 lines	b. 4 lines	c. 5 lines
5. **temperature**	a. +30	b. -30	c. 30°
6. **sheep**	a. weather	b. animal	c. location
7. **perfect**	a. no problems	b. no people	c. no feelings
8. **once every ____**	a. month	b. time	c. coin
9. **make a speech**	a. talk to group	b. cook for group	c. visit group
10. **cheat**	a. at a library	b. on a test	c. in the bay
11. **cherry**	a. red fruit	b. white fruit	c. yellow fruit
12. **throw away**	a. an old item	b. an expensive item	c. a perfect item
13. **car accident**	a. car purchase	b. car crash	c. car suggestion
14. **aquarium**	a. birds	b. fish	c. soccer
15. **cash**	a. my watch	b. my shoes	c. my money
16. **choose**	a. column	b. select	c. exact
17. **date**	a. March 31, 1999	b. 23 + 50 = 73	c. one year budget
18. **died**	a. not alive	b. not column	c. not born
19. **nephew**	a. male	b. female	c. male or female
20. **I'm pleased to ____**	a. meet you	b. be sick	c. go now
21. **younger than 12**	a. male	b. child	c. adult
22. **I'm in touch ____**	a. near the bank	b. with a car	c. by email
23. **plants**	a. kitchen	b. sharing	c. garden
24. **provide**	a. know	b. wear	c. give
25. **throw ____**	a. the ball	b. the weather	c. the shower

MORE VOCABULARY PRACTICE ON THE WEB

Go to the activities for unit 6 at www.press.umich.edu/esl/compsite/ targetinglistening/ and do the five vocabulary exercises there. Record your scores here. The best score in each exercise is 20.

Quiz 6.1. Your Score _____ / 20 _____

Quiz 6.2. Your Score _____ / 20 _____

Quiz 6.3. Your Score _____ / 20 _____

Quiz 6.4. Your Score _____ / 20 _____

Quiz 6.5. Your Score _____ / 20 _____

Exercise
1

Listening Activity: Taking a Test about International Tourist Destinations

Part 1 This is a test. Take a few minutes to match the tourist cities in the left column with their country or country and state in the right column.

International destination	Where is it?
____ 1. London	a. Turkey
____ 2. Bangkok	b. Brazil
____ 3. Honolulu	c. Kenya
____ 4. Auckland	d. Jamaica
____ 5. Cancun	e. England, U.K.
____ 6. Rio de Janeiro	f. Florida, USA
____ 7. Cairo	g. China
____ 8. Vienna	h. Hawaii, USA
____ 9. Orlando	i. Egypt
____ 10. Shanghai	j. Thailand
____ 11. Nairobi	k. Austria
____ 12. Kingston	l. New Zealand
____ 13. Istanbul	m. Costa Rica
____ 14. Cape Town	n. South Africa
____ 15. San José	o. Mexico

Part 2 Now listen to the information that you will hear to correct your answers. How many did you get correct? How much do you know about international tourist spots?

Dictation in a Dialogue: Finding the Best Airfare

This is a dialogue about a trip. The people in the dialogue are two friends discussing a short trip.

There are seven blank lines in the dialogue. Fill in each blank line with the correct sentence that you will hear.

Listen carefully. You will hear a number. Find that sentence number. You will hear each sentence three times. First, listen to the sentence. Repeat the sentence. Then listen again. Write the sentence. Finally, listen again. Check your sentence. The number in the parentheses is the number of words in the sentence. Now, let's begin with number 1.

Carl: I found a price from Orlando to Honolulu for $800 round-trip.

Trina: Wow! That's a great price. Where did you find it?

Carl: ❶ _____ (8)

Trina: Could you tell me the address?

Carl: Sure. It's **www.IlovetoFly.com.**

Trina: ❷ _____ (7)

Carl: Yes, I bought my ticket for my cousin's wedding last year.

Trina: ❸ _____ (4)

Carl: It was in Puerto La Cruz, Venezuela.

           ❹ _____ (7)

Trina: Was the weather hot? I always think South America is hot.

Carl: ❺ _____ (9)

Trina: ❻ _____

           _____ (11)

Carl: Yes, I bought them on Margarita Island. The price was great because there's no tax on the island.

Trina: ❼ _____ (6)

Carl: It was! I had a great time on this trip.

Extra Practice. **Listening Practice**

Close your books. Listen to the complete dialogue from Exercise 2. If there is any part that you cannot understand well, listen to that part again. (Try to listen to this dialogue without looking at your book. This is a good way to improve your listening.)

Extra Practice. **Dialogue Practice**

Work in pairs. Look at Exercise 2 again. Each person will be one of the characters in the dialogue. Read the dialogue as the characters. When you have finished, change characters and read it again. After you have finished, you may want to listen to the recording of the dialogue one more time.

Other Question Words	
It is important for you to know these four question words: ***who, what, when,*** and ***where***.	

Who	The answer to this question is the **name of a person or names of people**.	
	Who is your teacher?	Mr. Brown
	Who helped you?	Jimmy and Lim
What	The answer to this question is a **thing**.	
	What does she study?	Computers.
	What are you eating?	Scrambled eggs.
When	The answer to this question is a **time**.	
	When did you go there?	Last night.
	When is your birthday?	October 9th
Where	The answer to this question is a **place**.	
	Where do you live?	On Green Street.
	Where was your book?	On the kitchen table.

Exercise 3

Answering *wh-* Questions about Travel

Listen carefully to the questions that you will hear. Pay close attention to the first word of the question. Read the three choices, and then select the answer for the question. Circle the letter of your answer.

1. a. to Mexico
   b. with my sister
   c. in a small car

2. a. some medicine
   b. about five people
   c. about $500

3. a. many large planes
   b. without lunch
   c. in the capital

4. a. at the park
   b. in February
   c. with Yuko

5. a. the bus route
   b. at school
   c. two teachers

6. a. Ms. Alvarez
   b. next to the mall
   c. the doctor

7. a. near the bank
   b. at the front
   c. very much

8. a. next to my hotel
   b. from my travel agent
   c. to go to Paris, France

9. a. to Korea next summer
   b. very early in the morning
   c. a Korean-English dictionary

10. a. to arrive at the airport on time
    b. in my jacket pocket
    c. U.S. citizens need a passport to go there

Exercise

4

Speaking/Discussion: Talking about a Dream Vacation Destination

Practice 4A. Preparation

If you could travel any place in the whole world and stay there for ten days, where would you go? Write three specific reasons for choosing this destination.

_____

_____

_____

_____

_____

_____

_____

Practice 4B. Group Speaking/Discussion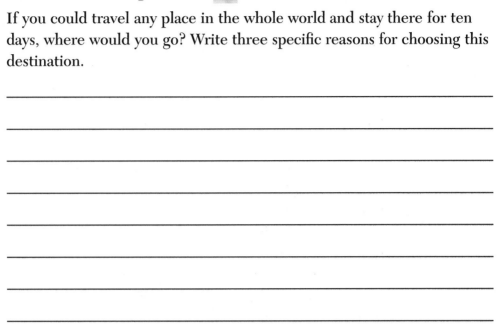

Now work with a partner or in a small group of three to four students. Take turns discussing your responses to the question in Practice 4A. Based on the discussion and reasons that you hear, which student do you think has the best dream destination?

Ordinal Numbers

1st	first	21st	twenty-first
2nd	second	22nd	twenty-second
3rd	third	23rd	twenty-third
4th	fourth	24th	twenty-fourth
5th	fifth		
6th	sixth	30th	thirtieth
7th	seventh	31st	thirty-first
8th	eighth	32nd	thirty-second
9th	ninth	33rd	thirty-third
10th	tenth	34th	thirty-fourth
11th	eleventh		
12th	twelfth	88th	eighty-eighth
13th	thirteenth	89th	eighty-ninth
14th	fourteenth	90th	ninetieth
15th	fifteenth	91st	ninety-first
16th	sixteenth	92nd	ninety-second
17th	seventeenth	93rd	ninety-third
18th	eighteenth	94th	ninety-fourth
19th	nineteenth		
20th	twentieth		

Rules for Ordinal Numbers:

(1) Numbers that end in **1** are **first**, **2** are **second**, and **3** are **third**.

   EXCEPT: 11 eleventh, 12 twelfth, and 13 thirteenth

(2) All other numbers end in **th**.

   REMEMBER! It is common to see letters **st, nd, rd,** and **th** with ordinal numbers.

Exercise
5

Recognition of Ordinal Numbers

Listen carefully. In this exercise, you will hear one ordinal number. The number will be repeated. Write the number in numeral form that you hear. Be sure to include the letters **st, nd, rd,** or **th**.

Example: YOU HEAR: "twenty-third"

ANSWER: _____23rd_____

1. _____   11. _____

2. _____   12. _____

3. _____   13. _____

4. _____   14. _____

5. _____   15. _____

6. _____   16. _____

7. _____   17. _____

8. _____   18. _____

9. _____   19. _____

10. _____   20. _____

Recognition of Cardinal and Ordinal Numbers

Listen carefully. In this exercise, you will hear a sentence that contains a cardinal or an ordinal number. Write the number in numeral form that you hear. Be sure to include the letters **st, nd, rd,** or **th** if you hear an ordinal number.

1. _____	6. _____	11. _____
2. _____	7. _____	12. _____
3. _____	8. _____	13. _____
4. _____	9. _____	14. _____
5. _____	10. _____	15. _____

Exercise

7

Understanding Simple Conversations: In a Travel Agency

You will hear a short conversation between a customer and a travel agent. The customer called the travel agent to ask about an airline ticket. Listen carefully. After you hear the conversation, choose the correct answer for each question and put a check (✓) on the line.

1. Where is the passenger going?
   ___ a. Miami
   ___ b. Houston
   ___ c. New York

2. How much did this ticket cost?
   ___ a. $119
   ___ b. $216
   ___ c. $150

3. What is the passenger's last name?
   ___ a. Paulman
   ___ b. Pasinpaul
   ___ c. Pollman

4. When does the flight arrive?
   ___ a. 9:10
   ___ b. 11:15
   ___ c. 11:50

5. What is the date of the flight?
   ___ a. November 4
   ___ b. October 4
   ___ c. November 11

Exercise
8

Anticipation

If you want to understand people when they speak English, it is important to listen very carefully. Sometimes you can understand people because you know what people will say before they speak. To **anticipate** means to expect or believe something will happen. For example, your friend walks into the room and he says, "I walked for three hours!" You can anticipate that he will also say, "I'm tired" or "My feet hurt."

In this exercise, you will hear one or two sentences. The last word is missing. You will finish the sentence with a word that completes the sentence well. Each sentence will be repeated. Do you understand? Now, let's begin with number one.

1. _____
2. _____
3. _____
4. _____
5. _____
6. _____
7. _____
8. _____
9. _____
10. _____

Exercise
9

Speaking/Discussion: Making Suggestions for a Great Trip

Practice 9A. Preparation

Traveling is exciting, but good preparation makes a good trip great. It is important to know about the weather and holidays in a place before you go there. For example, during Thailand's summer rainy season, it rains almost every single day. Knowing this simple weather fact may change your travel plans to Thailand! New York City in July is very hot. A family with small children might not want to go to New York City in July. Traveling to a city or country during a holiday can make travel more difficult.

Now imagine that someone is going for the first time to visit a country or city that you know well. The trip will be in the middle of August. This person does not know much of the language and has not traveled too much. What are five suggestions that you have for this person? (For example, you might write, "Be sure to bring an umbrella because it rains a lot in August.")

Travel destination: _____ (a place you know well)

1. _____

_____

2. _____

_____

3. _____

_____

4. _____

_____

5. _____

_____

Practice 9B. Group Speaking/Discussion

Now work with a partner. Take turns presenting your suggestions for a first-time visitor to your selected destination. Are there any similarities in your suggestions and your partner's suggestions?

Exercise
10

Following Directions (rows and columns)

Listen carefully to the instructions. Find the correct square. Write the correct information in the square. The first square is already completed for you.

	lesson	

Following Directions (rows and columns)

Listen carefully to the instructions. Find the correct square. Write the correct information in the square. The first square is already completed for you.

		listen

Listening Activity: Completing a Travel Itinerary

Kathy Williams is traveling to three cities. Here is her itinerary. Listen to this conversation between Kathy and her sister Rose. Listen to the information and fill in the missing pieces to Kathy's itinerary.

DATE	FROM	TO	PURPOSE
March 31	Miami	Dallas	
		San Francisco	Visit aunt and uncle
April 6	San Francisco		
			return home

Exercise 13

Sound Practice: /l/ and /r/ within Words

This is a rapid exercise. You will hear one word. Write the letter **L** or the letter **R** on the line to indicate the sound that you hear in that word.

Example: YOU HEAR: "red"

ANSWER: __R__

Beginning	**Middle**	**End**
1. _____	9. _____	14. _____
2. _____	10. _____	15. _____
3. _____	11. _____	16. _____
4. _____	12. _____	17. _____
5. _____	13. _____	18. _____
6. _____		19. _____
7. _____		20. _____
8. _____		

For extra practice, can you think of more examples?

Beginning	**Middle**	**End**
1. _____	4. _____	7. _____
2. _____	5. _____	8. _____
3. _____	6. _____	9. _____

Exercise
14

Sound Practice: /l/ and /r/ (minimal pairs in sentences)

Look at the list of words below. You will hear a sentence that has one of these words. Circle the word that you hear.

Example: YOU HEAR: "heel"

ANSWER: here

(heel)

1. light
   right

2. ball
   bar

3. long
   wrong

4. collect
   correct

5. cold
   cord

6. tail
   tear

7. glass
   grass

8. light
   right

9. bowling
   boring

10. he'll
    hear

Exercise 15

Understanding Simple Conversations: Traveling to Watch a Sports Event

You will hear a short conversation between two friends. They are talking about traveling to a championship basketball game. Listen carefully. After you hear the conversation, read the questions below. Choose the correct answer and put a check (✓) on the line.

1. Jennifer studied
    ___ a. two hours.
    ___ b. four hours.
    ___ c. eight hours.

2. Her test was in
    ___ a. French.
    ___ b. Geography.
    ___ c. History.

3. Jennifer studied
    ___ a. at the library.
    ___ b. at home.
    ___ c. in her class.

4. The game is
    ___ a. today.
    ___ b. this evening.
    ___ c. tomorrow.

5. Sarah will go to
    ___ a. Jennifer's house.
    ___ b. the library.
    ___ c. history class.

Exercise
16

Understanding Simple Lectures: Jet Lag

You will hear a short lecture. This lecture is about reducing the effects of jet lag. Listen carefully. After you hear the lecture, read the questions below. Choose the correct answer and put a check (✓) on the line.

1. How do people often get jet lag?
   ___ a. if they exercise while traveling
   ___ b. if they eat low-fat food
   ___ c. if they travel very far

2. What is the best liquid to drink?
   ___ a. vegetable juice
   ___ b. water
   ___ c. some type of hot liquid

3. Which type of food should you eat on the plane?
   ___ a. energy food
   ___ b. low-fat food
   ___ c. low-sugar food

4. When should you begin exercising?
   ___ a. during and after your flight
   ___ b. one day before your flight
   ___ c. two weeks after your flight

5. Why should you match your schedule with the local time?
   ___ a. the hotel's gym will be open
   ___ b. you won't have to change your watch
   ___ c. it will help you reduce your jet lag

Exercise 17

Pair Talking

Work in pairs. Student A works from this page, and student B works from page 194. Take turns describing the pictures with a dot; your partner can listen and ask questions to identify the correct picture and place a dot by the correct picture. Student A describes questions 1, 3, and 5, which are on this page. Student B describes questions 2, 4, and 6, which are on page 194.

A

1.

2.

3.
1. ✓	1. ✗	1. ✗	1. ✗
2. ✗	2. ✓	2. ✗	2. ✓
3. ✗	3. ✗	3. ✓	3. ✓
4. ✓ 50%	4. ✓ 50%	4. ✓ 50%	4. ✗ 50%

4.
✓	car		✓	call		✓	car		✓	call
a	are		a	R		a	are		a	R
17	70		17	70		17	70		17	70

5.

6.

B

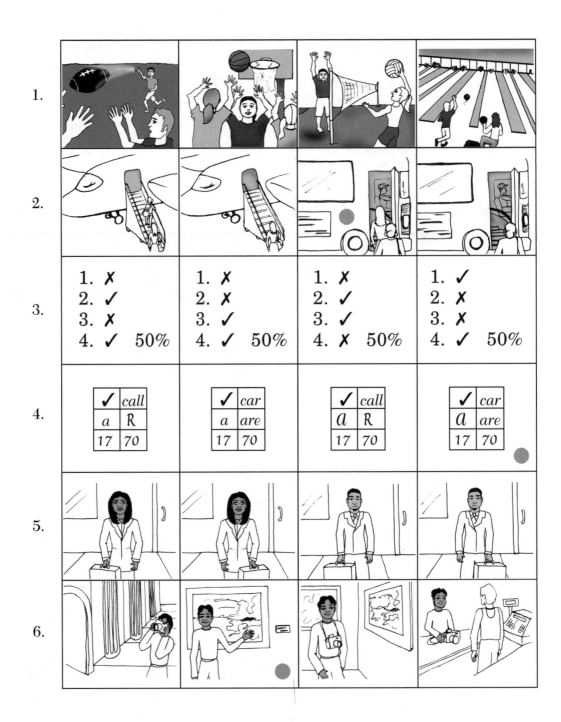

Exercise
18

Speaking/Discussion: Planning a Trip to an Exotic Destination

Practice 18A. Preparation

Work with a partner. The two of you will do some simple research (perhaps on the Internet) to plan a ten-day trip to one of these destinations:

- Ushuaia, Argentina (the very southernmost point of South America)
- Phuket, Thailand (a very nice beach resort)
- Cairo, Egypt (near the pyramids)
- Anchorage, Alaska (explore this great wilderness)
- Oslo, Norway (explore the fjords of Norway)
- Johannesburg, South Africa (a safari to Kruger National Park)

a. Travel: What is the cheapest flight for this destination? How long is this flight? You may want to use the Internet to get this information.

_____

_____

_____

_____

_____

b. What kinds of clothing would you take on this trip? It is important to travel light, so assume that you will have only one suitcase and one small carry-on bag. Include information about kinds of clothes, number of items, material (for example, cotton or wool). Don't forget shoes!

_____

_____

_____

_____

_____

c. How much money do you think that you would need for three meals per day in these cities? What kind of food do you expect to eat?

_____

_____

_____

_____

_____

d. What are some of the things that you will do at this destination?

_____

_____

_____

_____

_____

Practice 18B. Group Speaking/Discussion

Now take turns working in small groups of four to six students. (Alternatively, if the class is not very big, then pairs could make their presentations to the whole class.) You should take turns presenting your answers from Practice 18A. The students who are listening should ask questions if there is something that is not clear.

Exercise 19

Rapid Vocabulary Review

From the three answers on the right, circle the one that **best explains, is an example of,** or **combines with** the vocabulary word on the left.

VOCABULARY	ANSWERS		
1. **suitcase**	a. travel	b. spring	c. spots
2. **destinations**	a. times	b. events	c. places
3. **direct flight**	a. Ⓐ→Ⓩ	b. Ⓐ→ K →Ⓩ	c. Ⓐ→ G → P →Ⓩ
4. **far**	a. U.S. to Mexico	b. U.S. to Canada	c. U.S. to China
5. **championship**	a. sports	b. colors	c. travel
6. **fare**	a. flight time	b. flight cost	c. flight date
7. **for** _____	a. instance	b. ferry	c. already
8. **furthermore**	a. and	b. but	c. or
9. **an Internet** _____	a. overseas	b. Web site	c. jet
10. **itinerary**	a. attendant	b. schedule	c. instance
11. **jet lag**	a. tired	b. happy	c. expensive
12. **make a** _____	a. grass	b. reservation	c. break time
13. **match**	a. go together	b. throw away	c. fill in
14. **one-way**	a. street	b. bank	c. snack
15. **owl**	a. fish	b. bird	c. insect
16. **passenger**	a. in a class	b. in a bus	c. in a park
17. **passport**	a. travel	b. spring	c. store
18. **reduce**	a. +	b. 2×	c. −
19. **round-trip**	a. A → B	b. A → B → A	c. A → B → C
20. **snack**	a. apple	b. lunch	c. salt
21. **island**	a. in the bay	b. in the mountain	c. in the stretch
22. **clothes**	a. shirt, pants	b. cats, dogs	c. January, February
23. **war**	a. 2 countries	b. 2 tables	c. 2 agencies
24. **address**	a. of a place	b. of a flight	c. of a month
25. **century**	a. 60 minutes	b. 28 days	c. 100 years

MORE VOCABULARY PRACTICE ON THE WEB

Go to the activities for unit 7 at www.press.umich.edu/esl/compsite/ targetinglistening/ and do the five vocabulary exercises there. Record your scores here. The best score in each exercise is 20.

Quiz 7.1. Your Score _____ / 20 _____

Quiz 7.2. Your Score _____ / 20 _____

Quiz 7.3. Your Score _____ / 20 _____

Quiz 7.4. Your Score _____ / 20 _____

Quiz 7.5. Your Score _____ / 20 _____

Comprehension Checks

This unit consists of four multiple-choice quizzes. **Listening Comprehension A** should be done after one-fourth of the term is up, **B** after one-half is over, **C** after three-fourths is over, and **D** at the end of the course.

LISTENING COMPREHENSION A

You will hear a question. Read the three choices and then select the answer. Circle the letter of your answer.

1. a. Yes, it was.
   b. Yes, it does.
   c. Yes, it is.

2. a. Yes, he was.
   b. Yes, they are.
   c. Yes, they were.

3. a. 10
   b. 4
   c. 24

4. a. at the bank
   b. in the morning
   c. four hours

5. a. two hours
   b. at night
   c. in bed

6. a. Yes, I do.
   b. Yes, it is.
   c. Yes, we did.

7. a. No, they aren't.
   b. No, it isn't.
   c. No, she wasn't.

8. a. 11
   b. 24
   c. 5

9. a. a few
   b. a little
   c. Fine, thank you.

10. a. No, it wasn't.
    b. No, it doesn't.
    c. No, it isn't.

11. a. 15
    b. the green one
    c. only $13

12. a. Fine, thanks.
    b. 17
    c. at home

13. a. Yes, they do.
    b. Yes, it does.
    c. Yes, he did.

14. a. about 2 miles
    b. yesterday
    c. for 3 months

15. a. 550
    b. 515
    c. 505

16. a. Yes, I did.
    b. Yes, I was.
    c. Yes, I am.

17. a. No, it isn't.
    b. No, it didn't.
    c. No, it doesn't.

18. a. a few
    b. a little
    c. not much

19. a. last Wednesday
    b. home
    c. none

20. a. Yes, I am.
    b. Yes, I do.
    c. Yes, I did.

21. a. 80
    b. 2
    c. 18

22. a. Yes, I did.
    b. Yes, I do.
    c. Yes, I was.

23. a. 40 years old
    b. 40 miles
    c. 40 years ago

24. a. to the store
    b. last night
    c. Uncle Mark and Aunt Helene

25. a. Yes, he is.
    b. Yes, he did.
    c. Yes, he does.

You will hear a question. Read the three choices and then select the answer. Circle the letter of your answer.

1. a. a few
    b. a little
    c. very fine

2. a. 440
    b. 404
    c. 414

3. a. Yes, he was.
    b. Yes, he did.
    c. Yes, he does.

4. a. No, we don't.
    b. No, we aren't.
    c. No, we didn't.

5. a. 2 blocks
    b. 2 people
    c. 2 cars

6. a. 6
    b. 40
    c. 14

7. a. Yes, it does.
    b. Yes, it is.
    c. Yes, it was.

8. a. Yes, I do.
    b. Yes, I did.
    c. Yes, I was.

9. a. my brother-in-law
    b. in a car
    c. last week

10. a. No, she isn't.
    b. No, it isn't.
    c. No, he doesn't.

11. a. 30 years old
    b. 30 years ago
    c. 30 days

12. a. Yes, it is.
    b. Yes, it did.
    c. Yes, it was.

13. a. 2
    b. 10
    c. 24

14. a. a lot
    b. many
    c. none

15. a. Yes, he was.
    b. Yes, they were.
    c. Yes, she did.

16. a. two hours
    b. at 10 o'clock
    c. last night

17. a. Yes, I am.
    b. Yes, we are.
    c. Yes, it is.

18. a. last week
    b. in the morning
    c. at the supermarket

19. a. Yes, they do.
    b. Yes, we do.
    c. Yes, you do.

20. a. tennis and football
    b. every afternoon
    c. in the park

21. a. No, it isn't.
    b. No, it doesn't.
    c. No, it wasn't.

22. a. Yes, they do.
    b. Yes, it does.
    c. Yes, she does.

23. a. about 7 years old
    b. Fine, thanks.
    c. the green one

24. a. 4
    b. 8
    c. 12

25. a. this one
    b. blue and green
    c. about $25

Listening Comprehension C

You will hear a question. Read the three choices and then select the answer. Circle the letter of your answer.

1. a. at home
   b. right now
   c. Fine, thanks.

2. a. No, I didn't.
   b. No, I wasn't.
   c. No, I don't.

3. a. Yes, we are.
   b. Yes, we were.
   c. Yes, we do.

4. a. Aunt Agatha
   b. last night
   c. around 10 P.M.

5. a. 3 blocks
   b. the third one
   c. 3 days ago

6. a. Yes, it does.
   b. Yes, they do.
   c. Yes, he is.

7. a. 1
   b. 7
   c. 12

8. a. 10 pages
   b. at 10 P.M.
   c. 10 hours

9. a. 5
   b. 9
   c. 14

10. a. Yes, they do.
    b. Yes, it has.
    c. Yes, it does.

11. a. No, they weren't.
    b. No, I wasn't.
    c. No, I don't.

12. a. in a hotel
    b. only yesterday
    c. for 5 hours

13. a. 60 years old
    b. for a few days
    c. a long time

14. a. Yes, it was.
    b. Yes, it is.
    c. Yes, it does.

15. a. in the evening
    b. at the park
    c. five times

16. a. Yes, she was.
    b. Yes, they are.
    c. Yes, they were.

17. a. Yes, I was.
    b. Yes, I do.
    c. Yes, I am.

18. a. 808
    b. 880
    c. 818

19. a. No, he didn't.
    b. No, he wasn't.
    c. No, he doesn't.

20. a. a few
    b. a little
    c. sometimes

21. a. No, it isn't.
    b. No, it wasn't.
    c. No, it doesn't.

22. a. Yes, it did.
    b. Yes, it does.
    c. Yes, it was.

23. a. 1
    b. 20
    c. 9

24. a. only $12
    b. Fine, thanks.
    c. the brown one

25. a. a few
    b. a little
    c. 15 years ago

You will hear a question. Read the three choices and then select the answer. Circle the letter of your answer.

1. a. Yes, she is.
   b. Yes, she does.
   c. Yes, she did.

2. a. Doctor
   b. today
   c. two stamps

3. a. 50 miles
   b. 50 years old
   c. 50 years ago

4. a. Yes, I do.
   b. Yes, I was.
   c. Yes, I did.

5. a. 19
   b. 7
   c. 34

6. a. Yes, I am.
   b. Yes, I do.
   c. Yes, I was.

7. a. last night
   b. a few
   c. home

8. a. about 6
   b. 6 years old
   c. 6 days ago

9. a. No, they aren't.
   b. No, it isn't.
   c. No, it doesn't.

10. a. Yes, I was.
    b. Yes, I do.
    c. No, I am not.

11. a. 303
    b. 330
    c. 313

12. a. for 2 people
    b. about 2 more miles
    c. only 2 days ago

13. a. Yes, they do.
    b. Yes, he does.
    c. Yes, it does.

14. a. at home
    b. 45 years old
    c. Fine, thanks.

15. a. the brown one

    b. for $20

    c. only 8

16. a. No, it doesn't.

    b. No, it wasn't.

    c. No, it isn't.

17. a. a few

    b. a little

    c. Fine, thanks.

18. a. 4

    b. 11

    c. 21

19. a. No, they aren't.

    b. No, it isn't.

    c. No, it wasn't.

20. a. Yes, we did.

    b. Yes, it is.

    c. Yes, I do.

21. a. for 5 hours

    b. at night

    c. on the road

22. a. at the store

    b. at 9 o'clock

    c. at 1601 Green Street

23. a. 1

    b. 9

    c. 20

24. a. Yes, she was.

    b. Yes, they were.

    c. Yes, they are.

25. a. Yes, you will.

    b. Yes, you did.

    c. Yes, you can.

Appendix of Vocabulary

Words

alphabet	however	quiz
at least	how many	reason
attend	huge	report
begin	improve	salary
best	information	the same
blank	instructor	schedule
business	issue	section
circle	kindergarten	short
confuse	last name	similar (to)
continue	lecture	single
conversation	library	this situation
debate	list	smaller
definition	long	spell
depend	the main _____	statement
different	married	support
directions	math	Thursday
the director	mine	tough
discuss	most	Tuesday
dislike	multiple-choice question	underline
each _____	necessary	a uniform
education	only	university
every _____	the opposite	vocabulary
example	parentheses	a way
free	part-time	Wednesday
full-time	prepared	week
full-time program	public	your opinion
the government	the purpose	
history class	quality	

Expressions

about this idea	have to (+ verb)
about 10 people	(be) in great shape
agree (with someone)	X is longer/smaller than Y
allow (someone to do something)	it takes _____ minutes to (+ verb)
ask (someone to do something)	so (+ adjective)
at least _____ pages long	spend (time)
get to (+ place)	what about _____ ?
a great deal of _____	

Unit 2

Words

absent	edge	midnight
add	egg	mix
age	enjoy	mixture
apart	envelope	Monday
apple	excellent	move
appreciate	expensive	next
assignment	famous	noodle
as well as	favorite	not yet
bake	few	nut
bakery	find	oil
bay	first	once
beans	flour	onion
because	fresh	on top
blended	fried	open
bowl	friend	order
buffet	glass	oven
butter	go ahead	paint
buy	good cook	park
cabbage	guarantee	patient
carrot	happen	pea
cause	harmful	peach
cheese	hear	percent
chef	heavy	pet
chicken	helpful	picture
children	huge	play
choice	iced tea	popular
chop	include	postcard
clean	influence	potato
clearly	ingredient	practice
coast	item	pretty
cookie	kitchen	pretty (+ ADJ)
count	later	pronounce
customer	lawyer	push
dance	lemon	rabbit
degrees	less	rare, medium, well-done
delicious	let	recipe
dentist	lettuce	refrigerator
dessert	lightly	represent
(be) on a diet	listen to	result
distinct	lot	rice
door	love	the right way
drop	map	room
dry	melted	salad
early	menu	sandwich

seafood
server
several
side item
snore
society
soup
stamp
start
step
strawberry
strong
success
successful
such as
sugar
suggest
supermarket
sure
sweet
take place
talk
there are
there is
thirsty
tip
tired

toasted
together
tomato
too
trip
try
tuna
turn on
typical
vacation
vanilla
vegetable
wash
a watch
watch TV
the wrong way
wave (at _____)
(be) well known (for _____)
wet
wheat
whether
window
wonderful
wood
would like
year
yolk

Expressions

as (quickly) as possible
Could you tell me …?
(be) good at (doing something)
How do you like your steak cooked?

I don't think so.
in a few minutes
in that case
X sounds good.

UNIT 3

Words

animal
announce
announcement
approximately
bark
bear
believe
bell
bird

blueberry
bone
brown
cat
ceiling
(be) close to
compared
corner
cost

cow
cross
deer
describe
dirty
dog
elephant
enough
escape

explain
face
the fall
fall asleep
foot (feet)
female
fingernail
finished
fish
a fly
fox
free
fun
get home (=arrive, idiomatic)
get up
got home (get home)
giraffe
hair
hamster
horse
human
imagine
inside
interesting
kangaroo
kind of
kitten
large
leave (left)
light (color)
loud
lying down
male
might
miss
motor
mountain
mouse
movie
near
nearby
negative
noise
noisy
obvious
obviously
office
outside

own
owner
parrot
permit
photo
piece
positive
prefer
pretend
price
puppy
quiet
repair
(be) right here
(be) scared (of _____)
sell
a shop
shy
sing
sleep
snake
south
special
spicy
spider
standing up
(be) suitable for
sweet
symbol
tail
toe
toenail
tooth (teeth)
treat
tropical
truck
turtle
unusual
variety
vet
veterinarian
weigh
what kind (of _____)
wild
wish
worry
yard
zoo

Expressions

I haven't seen you in a long time.
in a long time
X sounds like Y.

take a break
take a nap
What are you doing?

UNIT 4

Words

achieve	especially	poster
act	failed	to present
album	fuel	printed
alone	full (of _____)	probably
altitude	gift	proud of
amateur	go shopping	pulled
amazing	graded	puzzle
amount	grandmother	rain
antique	great	red
attended	great-grandmother	rob
beach	green	rocket
beat	the ground	season
become (became)	guess	select
believe	gym	send (sent)
belonged to	heat	slapped
between	highest	smoke
birthday	hobby	sports
bookstore	jar	stay (in a place)
borrow	label	strange
bottle	lake	subtract
bought	laugh	surf the Internet
can(s)	launch	surprised
capital	liquid	take a walk
carry	located	take up a hobby
child	lose	taste
clock	magazine	team
coin	mail	a toaster
collect	mall	touch
common	meal	trade
complete	mention	travel
convention	museum	tremendous
cough	newspaper	uncle
country	next to	use
crashed	over twenty	vacation
cry	pack up	visit
decide	parent	winner
dialed	party	wonderful
end	peeled	wondering
erase	popcorn	work out

Expressions

a long time ago
become interested (in _____)
How (adjective)?

How high?
I'm not sure.

UNIT 5

Words

addition	divide	multiply
advice	division	need
almost	equals	neighbor
a bargain	equal sign	news
to bargain	everything	pay
best	finally	plus
better	get along (with _____)	a purchase
birthday	gift	recommend
boss	graduate	save
budget	graduation	spend (money)
a case	high school	subjects
catch (caught)	item	suggest
comments	living room	take away
congratulations	low	ticket
consider	lower	times (×)
daughter	mathematics	tourism
a deal	money	usual
description	motorcycle	
destination	multiplication	

Expressions

(number) goes into (number)
How much is _____ ?
in hindsight
in other words

instead of
It's a deal.
What do you think of that idea?

UNIT 6

Words

accident	be born	cell phone
activity	bottom	cheat
alive	brother	a check
anything else	brother-in-law	cherry
aquarium	busy, busier, busiest	chew
arrange	cash	chin
ask for	cashier	choose
baseball	CD player	chose
beginning	celebrate	clue

column
cousin
dad
date
die (died)
draw
drive
email address
establish
evening
every other
exact
an exam
family
family name
farm
fill in
follow directions
forget (forgot)
friendly
friendship
garden
go camping
go well
grow, (grew)
grow (grew) up
guest
guy
height
holiday
honeymoon
hope
hotel
hurt
husband
ice
in ages
influence
influential
introduce

kids
(to) last
leader
left
let's
a letter
location
look alike
make a plan
make a speech
marbles
mash
May
member
middle row
mom
month
nephew
never
next month
niece
November
October
often
an only child
pass an exam
paycheck
people
per _____
perfect
plants
play pool
please
points
pounds
provide
race
relationship
remember
reunion

rich
right
right now
row
run (ran)
Saturday
(to) score
(the) score
senior
share
sheep
ship
shirt
show
shower
sister-in-law
slowly
soccer
specific
square
Sunday
tall
temperature
think
through ten
throw (threw)
throw away
T-shirt
vote
weather
wedding
weekend
welcome home
whole
wife
will
witch
word
young
younger

Expressions

Everything is going fine here.
Go to (a place) on business
have a chance to _____
How are you doing?
How have you been?

I haven't heard from you in ages!
I'll tell her that you called.
I'm doing great.
I'm pleased to meet you.
(Pleased to meet you.)

(be) in touch (with _____)
It is nice to meet you.
(Nice to meet you).
The last time that I saw Aunt Rita was in
    1999.
look forward to _____

once every _____
once every few years
(be) on vacation
What do you want on your pizza?
What is your last name?

Unit 7

Words

address	finger	owl
airport	flight	passenger
already	flight attendant	passport
anticipate	(to) fly	rate
April	foot (feet)	reduce
arrangements	for instance	round-trip
August	fruit	snack
basketball	furthermore	spots
berry	grass	spring
bowling	an Internet Web site	spring break
century	an invitation	store
championship	invite	stretch
cheap	island	suitcase
clothes	itinerary	summer
cord	jet	tax
cruise	jet lag	time zone
December	large, larger, largest	tourist
destination	lesson	travel agent
direct flight	make a reservation	traveler
effect	match	a travel guide
expect	muscle	very
far	neighboring	war
a fare	one-way	
ferry	overseas	

Expressions

Have you used that Web site before?
I called your house last night, but no one answered.
rare, medium, or well-done
See you later.
take someone to a place